Bigger Than the Box

Bigger Than the Box
The Effects of Labeling

Bonnie L. Haines

Unlimited Achievement Books
Oacoma, South Dakota

First printing 2004

ISBN 0-9728542-2-3
LCCN 2003102166

ATTENTION CORPORATIONS, UNIVERSITIES, COLLEGES, AND PROFESSIONAL ORGANIZATIONS: Quantity discounts are available on bulk purchases of this book for educational, gift purposes, or as premiums for increasing magazine subscriptions or renewals. Special books or book excerpts can also be created to fit specific needs. For information, please contact Unlimited Achievement Books, PO Box 105, Oacoma, SD 57365; (605) 734-4254.

In memory of my sister, Bette, who tried everything to overcome her "terminal" diagnosis, but lost the battle. Her will to live and overcome has been my continued inspiration.

Table of Contents

ACKNOWLEDGMENTS viii

PREFACE ix

INTRODUCTION 1

CHAPTER ONE
Labels—They're Not Just on Soup Cans Anymore 5

CHAPTER TWO
The Family Way 28

CHAPTER THREE
Me, Myself and I 49

CHAPTER FOUR
School Days 74

CHAPTER FIVE
Getting Personal 96

CHAPTER SIX
Hi, Society! 117

CHAPTER SEVEN
The Label's Off—Now What? 138

SOME FINAL THOUGHTS 159

INDEX 161

Acknowledgments

Writing a book requires a lot of help, and I am grateful to the many people who were so willing to provide it.

At the top of the list of helpers is Fiona Young. Without her, my ideas would still just be swimming around in my head. It was her dedication and commitment to the project that helped me achieve my goal of having a book in print. My ideas and concepts were very scattered and disjointed but Fiona helped bring meaning and uniformity to them.

I also need to thank Marilyn Ross and her staff for all the advice and guidance they provided throughout the project. I would not have been able to do it without them.

Lastly, I would like to thank all those who have influenced my life. Namely, my parents and siblings but also all the students, staff, and friends I have had the opportunity to work with and have as a part of my life. Your influence in my life has been immeasurable and has helped me to achieve goals I never dreamed were possible. All of you were absolutely essential to the success of this book!

Preface

A Note About Bonnie

As a student in junior high I remember thinking to myself, "I will never treat students this way!" It was the late sixties, and I had a seventh- and eighth-grade teacher who made a lasting impression on me—but not because of a positive experience. The teacher would give a test on Friday and when you returned to school on Monday, you would find out how *everyone* scored on the test because you would be seated according to your score. The F's and D's were up front by the teacher's desk while those who received A's were in the back rows. Each week the same students were seated in the front and back—I just hoped to be closer to the back than to the front of the class! Those students at the front were considered to be troublemakers, the dumb ones who needed to be watched; those in the back were the good, smart kids who could be trusted not to cause problems for the teacher.

I attended junior high before much was known about special education and learning disabilities. There were students in my class who would have benefitted from one-on-one services but never received more than the humiliation of always being seated in the front row.

Maybe it was a result of that experience that I have spent most of my life working with students and finding ways to help them feel better about themselves. After ten years of coaching high-school and middle-school teams, I coached fifth- and sixth-grade girls' basketball for one year. It was only one year because I didn't coach the way the school wanted me to or like the other coaches. I had thirty fifth- and sixth-grade girls who were playing basketball for the first time as a competitive team sport. Naturally there were girls with more advanced skills than others but that didn't change the way I coached. I coached not to win, but to teach skills and life lessons. Each girl was allowed equal playing time during a game and I would alternate the starters so each girl was able to start a game during the season.

Not surprisingly, we didn't win a single game. I was unable to determine from the girls—ages ten to twelve—who would be a bas-ketball "starter" and who would be a "scrub." I felt strongly each girl deserved an equal chance to prove herself and to improve, so each girl was a starter. This defied conventional logic and certainly con-ventional coaching.

I am number four in a family of six children. There are only eight years between the oldest and the youngest, so you can imagine the camaraderie and the rivalry. I felt a strong sense of competition be-tween myself and my younger sister, who was only fourteen and a half months younger than I. I always thought she was more athletic, popular, smarter…the list goes on. I knew everyone in my family was smarter than I because I had standardized test scores to prove it.

When I tried to prove to my parents I couldn't do things because I was dumb, I would show them how my scores were so much lower than my siblings'. My parents never let me hold on to that notion, but I would still try to use it when I needed an excuse. I know now why my scores were lower. It had nothing to do with being dumb. It had to do with the fact I was a slower reader and a perfectionist. I needed to make sure the answer to the question was correct before I would go to the next question. As a result of those experiences, I still find myself avoiding standardized timed tests.

These experiences and many others have influenced me and have been my driving force for change.

Introduction

I became interested in the subject of labeling as a result of my many years in education. I taught high school for five years and spent fifteen years working as a school counselor. I have worked the majority of my time on Indian reservations and witnessed firsthand the devastating effects of labeling.

The study I remember as having an impact on my thinking was the one in which brown-eyed children were told they were smarter than blue-eyed ones. Immediately, the brown-eyed students began doing better in school. A few days later, the students were told they had been misinformed, that it was the blue-eyed youngsters who were actually smarter. Quickly, the scores of the blue-eyed children rose above those of their brown-eyed classmates.

Words have the power to influence behavior, and I have worked with hundreds of students who have been influenced, both positively and negatively. I want to share my experiences with you in hopes we can work together to begin to eliminate the labeling, bullying, and stereotyping that so wound our young people.

This book is about labeling, name-calling, and stereotyping. There may be subtle differences in the meanings of the words, but in our fast-paced culture, most people don't have time for subtlety and the terms are used interchangeably. It explores what labeling is, why we do it, how we do it, and what the effects are on us as individuals, on our families, and in our schools and workplaces. Labels are thrust on us as individuals by others and by ourselves. Awareness helps bring about change. We'll talk about being sensitive to how often we use labels, using them in a more positive way, and discovering alternatives to labeling.

Each chapter opens with quotes from people of many disciplines—poets, artists, writers, all sorts of people—relating to the subject of the chapter. At the beginning of each chapter you'll find a story, riddle, or fable. Stories are part of all world cultures. I find them fascinating by themselves and valuable as teaching tools. You'll find more stories within the chapters as well. At the beginning of each chapter and scattered throughout you'll see *Eye Openers*. These are conversation starters aimed primarily at adults. Though this book is intended to be used by educators in the classroom, it's my hope it will also prove useful to parents and others working with young people. Eye Openers are prompts to generate discussions relating to various topics, all on the theme of labeling and name-calling.

I've created games and activities identified as *Try This*. With the possible exception of cut'n paste activities, they can be applied to most K–12 settings. Younger and older learners can often use the same activity by adapting it to suit the situation. The language and materials may be different but the message is the same: Active learning is preferable to passive learning. Teachers, of course, understand their students best and will know what is appropriate for them. It's true great minds think alike! Therefore, you may already be doing some of these activities in your class. Some, but not all, of the Try This activities include variations. They are all intended as springboards for your own creativity.

Whether we want to reach adults or children, somebody who's involved learns more effectively than someone who is sitting back and letting it come their way. The topic of overcoming labels is serious but the approach doesn't always have to be—particularly with children. If kids have fun learning, if we can involve them in storytelling and fantasy, we can deliver the message right where they live. If you are moderating an adult discussion group, try to get a sense of how far you can stretch the participants' imaginations. Adults are often reluctant to engage in fantasy but sometimes it only takes one brave soul to get things going.

Throughout each chapter you'll find a liberal sprinkling of true-life stories relating to the theme of the chapter. Some of them may strike a responsive chord. Perhaps you've had similar experiences. There's nothing like a, "That happened to me, too!" reaction to help us get together to solve problems. We gain strength in learning about what has happened to others and how they have handled similar experiences.

Introduction

To Think About prompts are similar to Eye Openers, in that their intent is to provoke thought on a particular point or issue. Giving them a different name is another way of bringing ideas to your attention.

It is my sincere hope you will find this book user friendly. Nothing seems to raise peoples' dander more than education issues. They rouse arguments even more quickly than discussions about religion. What I'd like to see is teachers, educators, and parents using the material here as a jumping-off point to begin solid dialogue on how to help overcome the stigma and hurt caused by labeling, particularly in schools. We need to really *listen* to our children. They're telling us important things. It would be nice to offer important things back to them.

Bonnie L. Haines
South Dakota, 2003

Chapter One

Labels—They're Not Just on Soup Cans Anymore

It takes two to speak the truth—one to speak, and another to hear.
—Henry David Thoreau

The tendency in this country to put labels on everything from people to political philosophies does a disservice to the individuality that is the strength of this nation.

—J. R. Abbe, senior editorial
writer, *Fort Worth Telegram*

The Wise Men and the Elephant

Once upon a time, there were six wise men who lived together in a small town. The six wise men were blind. One day, an elephant was brought to the town. The six men wanted to see the elephant, but how could they? Being wise men, and friends, they consulted together and devised a solution to the problem. They decided each of them would feel a different part of the animal and they would share their impressions to discover what an elephant looked like.

So the six men went to feel the elephant.

The first man touched the elephant's big, flat ear. He felt it move slowly back and forth. "The elephant is like a fan!" the first man cried.

The second man felt the elephant's big, sturdy legs. "No, no. He's like a tree!" he exclaimed.

"You're both wrong," said the third man, feeling the elephant's tail. "The elephant is like a rope."

Just then the fourth man pricked his hand on the elephant's sharp tusk. "The elephant is like a spear!" he cried.

The fifth man felt the elephant's side. "He's like a high wall."

The sixth man, holding the elephant's trunk, declared firmly, "You are all wrong. The elephant is like a snake."

"No, like a rope."

"Snake!"

"Wall!"

"You're wrong!"

"I'm right!"

The six blind men shouted at each other for an hour, each holding to his belief. Finally, exhausted, they went home. And they never found out what an elephant was like.

On March 5, 2001, a doe-eyed, slender boy of fifteen walked on to the campus of Santana High School in Santee, California, a community twenty minutes east of San Diego. Minutes later, a fourteen-year-old and a seventeen-year-old lay dead; thirteen others were wounded. By some accounts the shooter, Charles "Andy" Williams, was a happy, laughing boy…a good friend. Others say he was shy and withdrawn, unhappy and homesick for the friends he had left behind on the East Coast and an easy target for bullies because of his small size and quiet nature. By his own definition, he had been the target of merciless teasing. He had enough. And he snapped.

His shooting spree lasted eight minutes, during which time he reloaded his weapons four times. According to an off-duty police officer, who happened to be on campus and aided in apprehending Andy, the boy merely aimed at and shot anybody in his path. Although the shooting was apparently motivated by a toxic overdose of teasing, he did not take aim at his oppressors. He did not know either of the two boys he killed.

Two years before Andy's rampage at Santana, Barry Loukaitis, a junior high school student in Moses Lake, Washington, hid a shotgun under his trench coat and walked into his classroom. Fifteen minutes later, two students and a teacher were dead and another student was seriously wounded. The first boy he shot, a popular athlete who had often bullied the shooter, died instantly. Classmates described Barry as a shy and serious loner. He was a boy with few friends, who was a much-used target for harassment. His oversized feet, gangly build, studiousness, and cowboy clothing apparently made him ripe for bullying.

People say, "Sticks and stones will break my bones, but names will never hurt me." That's not true. Names do hurt. They hurt a lot.
—Middle-school boy

Is labeling any more prevalent than it was a generation ago? It's difficult to judge but, more and more, it seems to have deadly results. Violent crime has risen significantly in the past forty years, most of it committed by young people. Half of U.S. households now own firearms. Adolescents seeking vengeance for bullying, labeling, and teasing are finding access to vengeance easier all the time.

Labeling is so much a part of human behavior, *labeling theory* has become a separate subject within the study of sociology. According to theory, labels placed on people may lead them to act the role associated with the label whether or not it is accurate. When others know a label, they may interpret the labeled person's behavior as abnormal, whether it is or not. Like most stereotypes, the generalizations of labels start from kernels of truth. There's usually just as much truth that belies the stereotype. We tend to construct meanings from situations. If those meanings don't fit with what we know, we take what is there and pound the square peg into the round hole.

We're labeled in our families by our parents, grandparents, siblings, or other family members. Labels can be assigned as a result of a quirk of personality or a dollop of talent. They can even stem from lack of talent.

I have to laugh when I read or hear something about oldest children and how they go into "structure" occupations like architecture or administration. It's like astrology, I guess. They make enough generalizations that it's got to apply to somebody. I got generalized enough by nature and by dint of being the oldest into to much re-

sponsibility too early. There are some things that are true about it. I'm an actor. Is that "structure"?

—Annie F.

The workplace is rife with labeling, such as the phenomenon known as *the glass ceiling* encountered by women. Our levels of education label us. We're labeled by age, in the workplace and in our everyday lives. Patients often complain that their doctors see them as their disease rather than a person who has the disease. Sexual orientation, religious affiliation, body type, body parts, ethnic group, profession and socio-economic status—anything can be a target for labeling.

I'll never forget the first time a store clerk called me "ma'am." I felt like I was about two hundred years old. When did I get to be a "ma'am"?! Ouch!

—Flora F.

Everybody has family stories. Before we go to school or get a job, we have family. It's one of the first places we're likely to get labeled. Often the labels stem from well-meaning family and are intended to bolster us but do the opposite. These follow us into adulthood. Some of us are able to discard them; others never outlive them but learn to live with them. A few are attached to us by accident of birth order. The youngest child will always be the youngest. Whether or not someone is able to shake off the tag of "baby" is up to him or her.

For many of us, our growing years were full of name-calling experiences. *Geek* is a popular label that used to be applied to an intellectually inclined child and is now applied to the computer-oriented child. *Tomboy* is a term applied to girls who like and are good at "boy stuff." Many of today's parents are actively trying to ensure that children of either gender are at least exposed to activities, which in the past, have been gender-specific (such as cooking for girls or wood shop for boys).

TRY THIS

Have your students act out the story of the six men and the elephant. (Because only seven students are involved in acting, have other students make a large painting of an elephant to tack up on the board.) Each of the six actors plays a different wise man, touching a different part of the elephant. If time permits, have other groups of actors perform the play. If interest is high enough, repeat the activity another day. For young children, repetition is extremely valuable.

In light of reading about the tragedy at Santana High School, think about this: According to psychology professor Robert S. Feldman, "The self-image we create in childhood causes us to continue in our adult lives to fit whatever labels we have accepted."

EYE OPENER

Do you believe Professor Feldman's assertion? What's the worst thing anybody called you when you were a kid? How did you react then? What strategies do you use now to deal with negative labeling?

When I was a kid, the worst thing anybody could call me was a liar. I hated it then and I still hate it. I mean really hate it. I had a fight with my best friend when I was about ten. She called me a liar, the way kids will, except like those characters say in the movies, "This time it's personal." It was mainly because she frequently did lie to me, so when she falsely accused me, I took it to heart and didn't talk to her for a while. We made up, like kids will. One day you're enemies and the next you're back to being best friends.

To this day, though, I still hate the label. There are real liars in the world, and I know who they are most of the time. I'm not one of them. Of course I wouldn't stop talking with somebody if they called me that. I'd sit down and talk with him or her—after I had myself under control. The word "liar" used in the wrong circumstances sets my teeth on edge and makes me clench my knuckles. I have learned not to fly off the handle. Maybe someday I will really grow up and not even react like this. For now, I'll settle for this.

—Joanne G.

If somebody calls me a liar, I get so mad I feel like punching them! I don't, because I'd get in trouble, but I sure want to. I don't tell lies. Well, hardly ever, anyway. Really. And I know some adults might think, "Oh yeah, he's just a kid. Kids tell lies all the time. He's probably just saying that because it sounds good." It's true, some kids do tell lies. Hey, that sounds funny, doesn't it?! But I don't. Sometimes adults don't believe you just because you're a kid, and that's not fair. Besides, if I did tell a lie, my mom would probably be able to tell. She knows me! That's a good thing; even a kid might think it's bad because you can't get out of trouble that way. You want to know what the good thing about that is? She believes me when lots of other people don't. And she hates people calling her a liar too, so she really understands how that feels.

—Devon, age twelve

Teasing, bullying, and name-calling—other names for labeling—have taken on an increasingly violent caste in the past few years. The tragedy that unfolded that morning at Santana High School had seemingly been set in motion for some time. Had Andy Williams' self-esteem been so badly damaged by the teasing he had endured, he merely lashed out beyond control?

Ironically, according to a former president of the American Psychological Association, many violent people—children and adults—have *high* self-esteem.

Why Do We Tease, Taunt, or Label?

Perhaps the biggest question asked about teasing is, why? Teasing, suggesting gentle verbal play, is more accurately termed taunting, which better describes what's going on. We are a nation of speed. Labeling or stereotyping equals speed. In our desire to do more and do it faster, we categorize everyone and everything. And we do it quickly. We meet someone; we want to assess them immediately. We slap on a label: white, black, female, male, jock, suit, nerd— whatever seems to fit. The media helps contribute to this by feeding an apparently insatiable appetite for sound bites. If an Internet site doesn't load quickly enough, we're off and running to the next one. If we have to wait for more than five minutes, we shift lines at the supermarket. The word *stereotype* comes from the process of making metal plates for printing and means "a set image." Applied to people, stereotype means an "instant or fixed" picture of a person or a group of people. A stereotype is based on an oversimplified or mistaken attitude, opinion, or judgment. Oversimplifying can't help but lead to misunderstanding.

TRY THIS

One of the funniest, silliest games going is the Slow Race. Divide the group into teams. The object is to go s-l-o-w-l-y. The *last* team to finish wins. Sometimes kids have a hard time grasping this concept. It's a game that usually ends in giggles.

I was very uncoordinated when I was a kid. My mother razzed me endlessly about it. She called me "handless." She acted like it was just teasing. Maybe to her it was but she never let up and would tease me all the time. She had to be pretty tough and thick-skinned when she was a kid, and she expected all of us to be the same way, whether we really were or not. I wasn't, but I sure learned not to let on how much the teasing hurt. The names really hurt.

"Dummy" was tossed around all the time, even for minor mistakes. I won't let my kids even say that word. At some point, I know I just decided I could let go of the hurt, but the word was just too strong for me to deal with.

A younger sibling was very talented with her hands, and even though I longed to try some artistic kinds of things, I never would while I lived at home. For one thing, I knew my efforts would never compare with my sister's. That was okay with me, and it was okay with my sister. She liked the fact I was interested. What really stopped me was the thought of dealing with my mother's joking critique of my efforts, and the comparison I knew was inevitable. It took me years to realize I was just fine the way I was. Although I didn't have the natural talent others had, I could still do some things well if I just applied myself. I actually did have some elements of artistic talent. Even more importantly, the trying and doing was the single most important element in the enterprise anyway.

—Tracy K.

Television's influence on culture is profound. Here, too, stereotypes help feed the instant image fix we seem to crave. Because most TV shows are short, writers often take shortcuts. When westerns were popular, the good guys wore white hats and the bad guys wore black hats. It was quick, easy and neat. You knew instantly who was who and you didn't need to think much about it. As adults we can say, "It's only a TV show." However, many children, particularly the very young, get their life cues from such shows. What they see is real to them, even if parents advise them (however, many do not) to the contrary.

Some cultural, ethnic and racial groups are almost invisible on television. When they do appear, in what context do they appear? Asians are usually depicted as servants, karate experts, Fu Manchu–type villains, or as the super-good, super-wise detective, Charlie Chan. Television dramas and sitcoms often depict minority characters as sidekicks supporting white actors in the leading roles—the characters who make decisions, solve problems, and usually hold positions of power. *The Cosby Show* during the 1980s was an exception to this trend. It depicted a stable, two-parent home run by two highly successful professional people.

Labels leave out more than they include. That's the whole point. They're quick. By themselves, or taken with a big pinch of salt, labels are relatively harmless. What harms is the value we place on them and often carry with us from the past.

Labeling and teasing has always been a part of growing up. "Kids are cruel," and "kids will be kids," are part of the mantra of parenting. Labeling, name-calling, and stereotyping, though subtly different, are variants on the same limiting way of looking at others and ourselves.

EYE OPENER

For older learners and adults: Do you think it's natural for children to be cruel to each other? Why or why not?

TRY THIS

Teachers, bring a "surprise box" to class. Have each child in the class write something they like about themselves on a piece of paper and put it in the box. Draw out slips during the day and read them aloud. Over the course of a few days or a week, everyone will have been acknowledged. Watch for students who are struggling to find something to say. Younger students might enjoy an approach like, "Someone likes the way he or she draws cats." The child who wrote the comment will get a kick out of knowing and will probably let on in some fashion. There's a good chance the rest of the class will know, too.

Labeling and name-calling make some people feel isolated and alone, particularly if they feel they have no support or nobody is listening. It's especially important to listen to children who complain their peers are calling them names, even if you think they might be exaggerating about the amount of the teasing or name-calling. You can always sort things out later. What counts when a complaint like that is made is *listening*.

TRY THIS

For younger learners (or adults who aren't shy!): You will need a variety of hats or costume clothing, preferably those that designate a profession, such as a fireman's helmet or a construction worker's helmet (these can often be found at thrift stores or yard sales). Toys can be substituted. With the class seated in front of you, ask them who you are. Very young children will find this silly. Of course they know who you are! Don an article and adapt a pose or mime an action that could be associated with the article. If you have a toy stethoscope, pretend to listen to a heartbeat. Ask the children, "Now who am I?" Some children may identify you as the new character, but most will not. Discuss appearances and labels and why externals cannot entirely define a person.

The Trumpeter Taken Prisoner

A trumpeter during a battle ventured too near the enemy and was captured by them. They were about to proceed to put him to death when he begged them to hear his plea for mercy.

"I do not fight," said he, "and indeed carry no weapon; I only blow this trumpet, and surely that cannot harm you; then why should you kill me?"

"You may not fight yourself," said the others, "but you encourage and guide your men to the fight."

What's in a word? A few months after George W. Bush had taken office, Senator Jeffords of Vermont changed his party affiliation from Republican to Independent, throwing off the balance of power in Congress.

"I will leave the Republican Party and will become an Independent," Jeffords said.

According to the senator, he felt he could no longer serve the people he represented with his Republican Party affiliation. Was he really *deserting* the people of Vermont? As might be expected, his action created political shock waves across the country. A radio report a few weeks later described his defection, defined as "a desertion from allegiance, loyalty, duty, or the like." Is that what the senator was doing?

"I have changed my party label," Jeffords said, "but I have not changed my beliefs."

From a strict party point of view the definition may fit, but it's a narrow definition. From the Senator's point of view, far from deserting his allegiance, he was strengthening it. Linguists call a word like *defection* a loaded word. It's a word with strong connotation. It's a word that makes a judgment. It's a word that labels.

Labeling crosses historical and cultural boundaries. The following story is Native American lore about labeling, *Turtle's Race With Bear*:

It was an early winter; cold enough so the ice had frozen on all the ponds and Bear, who had not yet learned in those days it was wiser to sleep through the White Season, grumbled as he walked through the woods. Perhaps he was remembering a trick another animal had played on him, perhaps he was just not in a good mood. It happened that he came to the edge of a great pond and saw Turtle there with his head sticking out of the ice.

"Hah!" shouted Bear, not even giving his old friend a greeting. "What are you looking at, Slow One?"

Turtle looked at Bear. "Why do you call me slow?"

Bear snorted. "You are the slowest of the animals. If I were to race you, I would leave you far behind." Perhaps Bear never heard of Turtle's big race with Beaver and perhaps Bear did not remember Turtle, like Coyote, is an animal whose greatest speed is in his wits.

"My friend," Turtle said, "let us have a race to see who is the swiftest."

"All right," said Bear. "Where will we race?"

"We will race here at this pond and the race will be tomorrow morning when the sun is the width of one hand above the horizon. You will run along the banks of the pond and I will swim in the water."

"How can that be?" Bear said. "There is ice all over the pond."

"We will do it this way," said Turtle. "I will make holes in the ice along the side of the pond and swim under the water to each hole and stick my head out when I reach it."

"I agree," said Bear. "Tomorrow we will race."

When the next day came, many of the other animals had gathered to watch. They lined the banks of the great pond and watched Bear as he rolled in the snow and jumped up and down making himself ready.

Finally, just as the sun was a hand's width in the sky, Turtle's head popped out of the hole in the ice at the starting line. "Bear," he called, "I am ready."

Bear walked quickly to the starting place and as soon as the signal was given, he rushed forward, snow flying from his feet and his breath making great white clouds above his head. Turtle's head disappeared in the first hole and then in almost no time at all reappeared from the next hole, far ahead of Bear.

"Here I am, Bear!" Turtle called. "Catch up to me!" And then he was gone again. Bear was astonished and ran even faster. But before he could reach the next hole, he saw Turtle's green head pop out of it.

"Here I am, Bear!" Turtle called again. "Catch up to me!" Now bear began to run in earnest. His sides were puffing in and out as he ran and his eyes were becoming bloodshot, but it was no use. Each time, long before he would reach each of the holes, the ugly green head of Turtle would be there ahead of him calling out to him to catch up!

When Bear finally reached the finish line, he was barely able to crawl. Turtle was waiting there for him, surrounded by all the other animals. Bear had lost the race. He dragged himself home in disgrace, so tired he fell asleep as soon as he reached his home. He was so tired that he slept until the warm breath of the Spring came to the woods again.

Not long after Bear and all the other animals had left the pond, Turtle tapped on the ice with one long claw. At his sign a dozen ugly heads like his popped up from the holes all along the edge of the pond. They were Turtle's cousins and brothers, all of whom looked just like him!

"My relatives," Turtle said, "I wish to thank you. Today we have shown Bear it does not pay to call other people names. We have taught him a good lesson."

Turtle smiled and a dozen other turtles, all just like him, smiled back. "And we have shown the other animals," Turtle said, "turtles are not the slowest of the animals."

TO THINK ABOUT

What's a *good* word? What's a *bad* word?

TRY THIS

Make a list of the words you would put in either "good word" or "bad word" categories.

Make a deck of cards using label words: fat, skinny, stupid, smart, etc. The dealer gives everyone a card and asks, "What does this word look like?" In small groups, younger learners can draw what they think the word looks like. In larger groups, the teacher can lead a discussion by pulling a card from the deck and asking the same question. Older learners can split into groups for discussion. They can do the same drawing exercise or create short skits illustrating the word.

One of the biggest problems created by labeling is it creates confining boxes that limit thinking and predetermine behavior. If you've been categorized as someone who couldn't do something, chances are you'll struggle to have the opportunity to do it, regardless of your ability. Once you're put in a box, you have walls around you. The same happens to someone else if you put them in a box.

My brother has been overweight his whole life. People would look at him and dismiss him immediately as never being an athlete. They couldn't have been more wrong if they tried. Coaches loved him. He wasn't Olympic caliber, but then how many are? One of the reasons they loved him was he was really good. He had excellent eye-hand coordination, which made him an excellent hitter in baseball. He wasn't the fastest base runner, but he wasn't the slowest, either. He put his head down and ran as fast as he could. Kids with much more athletic builds, the kind who were apt to label him "fatso" were often left in his dust. He had a decent arm for pitching; he was a good fielder because he paid attention, even when he was a kid, which lots of kids his age don't.

But you know one of the strongest reasons the coaches thought so highly of him? It was his attitude. There wasn't a better sport on the team than my brother; nobody was a bigger team player. He always tried his best, always supported his teammates and had the best time. He never let it get him down that other kids called him the "Pillsbury Dough Boy." He just laughed and poked himself in the belly. Even after all these years, when I get down on myself for something, or somebody tells me I can't do something, I'll remember him playing baseball. It helps get me past that point.

—Marla F.

My son was an absolutely terrific baseball player when he was a kid. I thought so, anyway, but I don't know a lot about the game except to observe which kids can catch, throw, and hit, and which kids can't. I used to volunteer in my kids' schools, too, so I was pretty good at spotting how the teams were working together or not. Sometimes I would sit in the stands and listen, not letting on I was his mom. I mean I was proud of him, but I did not want to be the obnoxious parent. So when other people said how good he was, I was just happy to hear it.

What made me even prouder, though, was when I'd hear from other parents about what a good team player he was. There was another kid on the team who was what's popularly referred to as a "hot dog." I heard some of the other boys walking home after games using this label. I'd talk to my son about not doing that, but I understood how the boys all felt. This kid frustrated them. He had lots of talent but no heart. He only cared about how well he did, not about the team, and he made no bones about that, either. He'd even say nasty things about one of the boys if he struck out or made a bad play. So although you don't like to hear kids talk like that, sometimes you can see how those things get started. Sometimes it's just sheer frustration.

—Paula P.

TRY THIS

You will need as many boxes as you have participants or teams (boxes should vary in size and shape) and a variety of objects to put in the boxes such as buttons, uncooked pasta of varying shapes, wrapped hard candies, poker chips, etc. Be creative.

Give each participant or team a box and give each box a name. Give each team large numbers of the objects, distributed evenly. Tell everyone to put as much as they can in their box. Those with small boxes won't be able to put as much in as those with bigger boxes. Discuss the names of the boxes. Have each person or group write down what they think is in the other boxes. Have the students talk about what's in their box. Relate what's in the box to what's outside the box. Discover how the labels the boxes have might influence what they thought was in the box.

Variation: Include in your list of objects small statuettes of people, make the boxes all the same shape and size. This time, instruct them to put all the things that *belong* in boxes into the box. The object, of course, is to leave the people *out*.

Name-calling links a person, or an idea, to a negative symbol, as does using negatively charged words. The person who does this is trying to get a reaction on the basis of that symbol. Words by themselves, obviously, can't hurt. They aren't good or bad. The problem is, they don't walk alone. Words carry meaning. Meaning comes from context, from the world around us. In our global society, John Donne's famous line, "No man is an island unto himself," takes on a bigger meaning than ever. Diverse cultures come into contact more and more.

A more subtle form of name-calling involves words or phrases selected because they possess negatively charged emotion. Someone opposed to budget cuts may characterize fiscally conservative politicians as *stingy*. Supporters might prefer to describe the same person as *thrifty*. Both words refer to the same behavior, but they have very different connotations. *Radical* is another example of a heavily charged word. Whether or not you see it as a negative depends on your perspective. The synonyms *sweeping*, *thorough*, and *far-reaching* sound much different than *radical*, don't they?

TRY THIS

Just for yourself: Read this list of words, then take a moment after each one and write down your thoughts as you read the word.

commie	fascist	pig	yuppie	bum	queer
(femi)nazi	dyke	biker	tycoon	ex-con	nerd

Now think of a more positive alternative for each name. Add more to the list.

Some Famous Nerds

- Steve Jobs, cofounder of Apple Computer
- Jeff Bezos, founder of Amazon.com
- Bill Gates, founder of Microsoft

TRY THIS

Have students make a list of all the names they've been called. Have them also make a list of the names they've called someone else. That list can be private, or shared in a way that removes the blaming aspect and lets it come up for discussion only. Discuss how it felt being called a name. What are the worst labels and why?

Another title for this book could well be *The Boy, the Girl, the Label, and the Self-Fulfilling Prophecy.* Labels can scar people for life. Studies have long shown that once someone has been labeled as a criminal the chances increase for that person to become the label.

TRY THIS

Construct a nonsense word that combines as many positive labels about yourself that you can get into a mouthful, like *goodwriterfastrunnerkindfunnyhappygirl.* This would work easily with a lesson on parts of speech. Students can use their invented words to make mini banners. Hang them up around the room. Add photos and you've got a good lesson and a good display item for back-to-school night.

TO THINK ABOUT

How many times have you said or heard "they said" or "they did" and wondered who *they* were?

TRY THIS

Take out a pencil and paper and make a drawing of *they*. You don't have to be an artist. *They* tend to help us close the lid on our boxes, to help us label ourselves. *They* can look like anything. Younger students might also make a collage using pictures from magazines.

EYE OPENER

The story of the wise men and the elephant illustrates the dangers of making judgments with incomplete information, or labeling. It's also a lesson on *anything by committee* where the group did not work from consensus. Can you think of any instances in your life where a project failed because of lack of cooperation? How would you handle that situation now?

An adult friend of mine with an unusual name had been teased about it when she was a child. It was a lovely name but not common where she lived. To make matters worse, she was very shy when she was young and suffered when the kids made fun of her name. When she got older, she had learned to appreciate how pretty her name was and to enjoy being different in that respect. She still found it difficult, sometimes, in very ordinary experiences. Cashiers at fast food places always gave her a double-take, she said. So she thought she'd make it easy on them. One day she ordered a hamburger and gave the cashier a very common name instead of her own. When "her" name was called, she wasn't listening for it and almost missed her order.

From then on, she gave her own name and let them deal with it. "I am who I am," she told me. "My name is different, but so am I. It isn't what makes me different, but it may have helped!"

—Sharon H.

TRY THIS

Have you ever wished you had a different name? Buy a package of wide labels. Have the kids pick a new name for themselves *just for the day*. Maybe your name is Lou and you've always wanted to know what it felt like to be Carlos. Encourage the kids to use their imaginations. Pick something as different from their own name as they can, even if it's a different gender—though that can really open up a can of worms! Have them be that name for a day. At the end of the day, talk about it. Did it feel different to be called another name? Does having a different name make *you* different?

(continued)

Note: Some children are unusually sensitive to activities like this. Allow these kids to opt out of adopting a different name if it evokes too much fear or other strong reaction against it.

TRY THIS

Labels are things you put on boxes and cans: Have each child bring in a can or two of food. Construct a box or receptacle to hold them. Remove the labels, coding the cans and labels so you can reattach them. Have the kids guess what's in each can. For younger learners, you can record the guesses on the board. Older children can do this in groups and record their guesses. Different sets of cans can be given to the groups and then rotated. Give everybody a chance to guess. If anybody gets lucky and guesses correctly, reward him or her with a sticker, pencil, etc.

Once the activity has been completed, have students help reattach the labels to the cans. Donate the cans to a local food bank.

Note: There may be a few children who can't bring, or forgot to bring, anything for this exercise, so be sure and have a few extra cans available.

A label is something others give to you. If you don't accept it, it isn't really yours. There are two ways to beat this type of social attack. You can *own* your label or you can *challenge* it. If you own the label, you can take any aspect of it that fits you and play it up, instead of the negative parts. If you choose to refute it, think hard about what might be true and play those aspects down. The primary goal, whatever choice you make, is to not respond to the jibes and become upset and frazzled. That is, after all, what they want when they select a target. If you don't give in, they don't win.

My son was a geek. He always was a geek, and he still is, and he's making a pretty good living being a geek. It never bothered him, or me. He was somebody who did better outside the system than in it. He taught himself about computers, hence the "geek" thing. Now he's using that knowledge and other people are consulting him. Labels aren't always a bad thing. You can turn them around to your benefit.

—Linda J.

I was labeled a talker when I was a kid because I always talked too much in class. Too much for the teacher to be comfortable with, anyway. She got tired of keeping me in at recess or hitting me on the knuckles with a ruler (in those days teachers were allowed to do that). One day she decided to put me in the choir because, like she told me, "At least there you can be moving your mouth and not get in trouble." (This was before the days when everybody had to be politically correct.) It worked. I still talked in class but not as much, and besides that, the choir teacher discovered I had a nice singing voice, which nobody knew before that.

—Brad F.

The old saying about a good offense being the best defense works for labels, too. Although we aren't advocating aggression, we are saying if labels are being thrown on you, act like it's no big deal. Don't allow someone else's words to get to you. Ignore it as best you can. Never let the labelers know they've hit the bull's-eye. Sometimes, too, labels can draw your attention to something you *do* want to change.

When I was in college, I worked in a department store. One night there were some kids hanging around late, when we were getting ready to close. They were really being obnoxious. I had to go to the other side of the store to get something for them and as I was walking away I heard them laughing at me, calling me a "hunchback." Naturally I was angry and hurt. I realized, later, they were right. I'd had sloppy posture most of my life. So I started paying more attention to it and improved my posture. Even now, years later, every once in a while, it comes back to me, and it's usually because I've been so busy I haven't thought about me. I take a breath and straighten up. It's good for my spine and it feels good to have something to show for feeling humiliated. They didn't win, I did!

—Maggie R.

Kids can be the most innocent and the meanest creatures, at the same time. They'll call a classmate, teammate, or friend a name, not realizing the hurt and confusion it can cause.

Labels—They're Not Just on Soup Cans Anymore

Not long after transferring to a new school, I found out my classmates were calling me a snob behind my back. This confused me, but I didn't do anything about it. I had a full year to catch up on in one subject, and I was a studious kid anyway. I didn't have time to worry about it. The "egghead" label I also picked up was something I could understand. Since I wasn't very good at the social stuff, it was something of a badge of honor for me. It wasn't until years later I understood what had been going on. I was a painfully shy adolescent and would retreat into my security zone—studies—all the time. What was for me just shyness was for my new classmates a "stuck-up" attitude. I found it nearly impossible to strike up conversations with new people. They thought I was being a snob. Once you've had that type of experience, it makes it easier to recognize it in somebody else—or it should, anyway.

A new colleague joined our staff, and I almost made the same mistake. Unlike many of our staff, she was very quiet and reserved, and didn't stop and chat even occasionally. She came from a very prestigious background, and it seemed at first, she was making sure we all knew that, but I stopped myself short one day. She's just a bit shy, I thought. It was atypical for the kind of work that was going on, but that's all it was, and in fact, on the occasions she does come out of her shell a bit, she's very sweet and funny—nothing like the image she normally projects.

—Cynthia W.

Kids cut to the chase quickly when they feel threatened or are confused about something or someone they don't understand. Name-calling with kids is a sling, but with adults it's an arrow. Grownups are more insidious with their name-calling. In the cases below, they have brought their labeling to the attention of the courts:

- A Washington state resident of Mexican-American ancestry brought suit in a case in which he claimed he had been humiliated and embarrassed by racial epithets directed at him by his fellow workers. He won his case.

- The town of Skokie, Illinois, tried to stop a pro-Nazi demonstration on the grounds it would cause harm to the many Jewish residents of the town, several of whom were Holocaust survivors. The court ultimately denied the claim, but not without making mention of a new basis in Illinois for filing such claims—namely, intentionally inflicting emotional distress. This case was lost only because first amendment issues took precedence. It's important, though, that the court agreed the demonstration, along with the display of Nazi swastikas and other symbols, would assuredly cause some people harm. Labeling people using racial terms will no longer be tolerated by the legal system.

TRY THIS

For older learners and adults: The Holocaust has continually been an issue that sparks impassioned debate. Ask your group how they would have decided whether or not to allow a pro-Nazi demonstration to take place? Students with enough background in U.S. history and some preparation can hold a Mock Court and try the case in the context of the classroom.

EYE OPENER

Would you describe the word *revisionist* as a label? Discuss history from a labeling point of view.

Labeling persists, in part, because to some extent we need it. Defining and labeling our experiences organizes our lives. It's where we get our ideas of good and bad, what we like and what we don't. When we look at these labels, we begin to get the idea our experiences aren't necessarily what shape us but rather how we *view* those experiences that does. Albert Einstein was often asked to explain his General Theory of Relativity. His classic response was if you held your hand on a hot stove burner for one minute, it would seem like an hour, but if you were spending an hour with a pretty girl, it would seem like a minute. Experiences are not necessarily one thing or another. How we label them is.

You never know just how much you set up your own windows on the world until someone else comes into it. I had a stepdaughter come to live with us and it took a long time before she came to an understanding of my humor. My kids and I had always tossed around names at each other that she was horrified to hear. For us, it was banter. We always knew when a situation had turned from joking to serious, but this poor girl didn't get it for quite a while. What we labeled normal, she labeled "mean." After a while, she learned, we learned. You adjust as much as you can because life can be pretty miserable if you are thrown into somebody else's system for organizing the world.

—Jeanie P.

Labeling gives us our handle on the world. When we see someone in a wheelchair, we don't need to know anything about them. We can call them "disabled" where we used to call them "crippled." Give something or somebody a name and you know all you need to know, just like when you see the white hat in the cowboy movie, you know that's the good guy. Here again, labeling limits perceptions. If a wheelchair signifies *only* an impairment the occupant has, you're closed to whatever the individual *can* do.

I worked as a respite worker for a local organization that provided relief for parents and other caregivers of children with all kinds of disabilities. One of the first clients I worked for had a young boy with severe cerebral palsy. When I walked in and saw this boy, I was really shocked. I'd never been so close to somebody who looked so completely out of it. It's uncomfortable for me to admit that as an adult I had this reaction, but I did. I tried not to show it; I don't know if I succeeded or not.

His mother was going over her instructions before she left and one of the things she asked me to do was to turn the TV to a particular channel at noon because her son enjoyed Perry Mason. I remember this so clearly. I was thinking, "Uh-huh. Sure he does. Like he can even tell." Understand, this boy was in a special wheelchair, his head flopped to the side, and he could not speak. I did as she asked, despite my doubts. That's when I had my second shock. The boy's demeanor changed sharply. He was paying attention. He really did like the show.

It was a humbling experience. I had come into this tiny apartment with all kinds of preconceptions, which were only reinforced when I saw the boy. I left a whole lot smarter and less judgmental. That boy taught me something. To this day I have never looked at anybody the same way again, and I'm really glad.

—Blair R.

Labeling helps us know what's normal. It orients us to our environment. When we know what *is* normal, we also know what *isn't*. From that we know who fits and who doesn't in our world. Of course the trouble with this idea is, although it's important for us to know who we are and where we fit in, there are just too many notions of what constitutes normal. Normal can't help but limit what we'll allow into our lives.

TRY THIS

For older learners: Divide the students into groups and arrange the groups so there's as much diversity as possible. Have them come up with an expanded definition of the word *normal*. Don't brainstorm ahead of time. Use this to generate a discussion. Some of what you are trying to elicit is group affiliation, age, race, grooming, dress, and demeanor.

Younger students can still talk about some of the concepts of *normal*. They can contrast their own neighborhoods with places that are different.

When I was a student teacher, I tried a variation of that famous experiment a classroom teacher did in the sixties—the one where she separated the class into the brown-eyed group and the blue-eyed group to demonstrate how racism gets started, and what happens to a society once it does. That experiment produced noticeable results. So did mine. It's a revelation to watch how selecting one criterion as the basis for discrimination can set up such powerful feelings. My students were surprised, too. They were much more sophisticated about such things than I was at that age, because these kinds of things are openly discussed now, and discussed often. Until you experience that arbitrary line, though, you can't really understand the incredible unfairness of being judged in that way. I caught some flack for it, but I'll bet you those kids won't forget.

—Jan D.

TRY THIS

As social norms change, so do our ideas of what's normal. Gather pictures from as many sources as possible, including historical ones. Hold up a picture of something obviously contemporary and ask, "Normal or not normal?" For younger learners, create a large two-column graph and paste the pictures into the columns and count the items. For older learners include some

—(continued)—

items, especially fashions, which could generate either response. Some retro fashions would be perfect for this activity. Talk about how the definition of normal changes according to the times.

Extra Credit: As an extension or variation, have students predict what will be normal in the future. Include as many categories as you can: food, fashion, behavior, intercultural (intergalactic?!).

How else can we create labels? Let's count the ways. Married or single? Veteran? Ex-con? Highly educated or just passed high school? Blue-collar or professional person? How do you make someone who falls into one of these categories, one you don't like, feel excluded? Simple. Make sure that person stands out as "out of the ordinary."

Labeling can be called a name game. The power of vision can't be underestimated, and there's no doubt names conjure images. Images are associated with labels, and people act on images. Sometimes the images are useful generalizations. Just as often they become stereotypes. Stereotyping seldom helps, it is more often hurtful. It hurts the person who does it. They don't grow or learn. It hurts the target; they've been stopped or limited by a shortened vision.

We can set several goals for our understanding of the labeling process: understand the labeling process, understand who is being labeled, understand who is doing the labeling, and understand the consequences of labeling.

TRY THIS

Gather pictures of different kinds of people. Strive for as much diversity as possible, of race and ethnicity, profession, lifestyle, and situation. Allow students only a short time to assign a one-word description to the picture. This can be done as a class activity or in smaller groups. In groups, ask for a consensus on the one-word descriptor. See how the interaction affects the choice. Allow for alternatives to be listed as well. Engage in a discussion as to how the choices were made.

On we go, now, to the beginning—the family.

Chapter Two

The Family Way

Parents are the last people on earth who ought to have children.
—Samuel Butler

They mess you up, your mum and dad.
They may not mean to, but they do.
They fill you with the faults they had
And add some extra, just for you.
—Philip Larkin

The Belly and the Members

One fine day it occurred to the Members of the Body they were doing all the work and the Belly was having all the food. So they held a meeting, and after a long discussion, decided to strike work till the Belly consented to take its proper share of the work. So for a day or two, the Hands refused to take the food, the Mouth refused to receive it, and the Teeth had no work to do. But after a day or two the Members began to find they, themselves were not in a very active condition: The Hands could hardly move, and the Mouth was all parched and dry, while the Legs were unable to support the rest. They found even the Belly in its dull quiet way was doing necessary work for the Body, and all must work together or the Body will go to pieces.

The old saying is you can pick your friends, but not your family. The family in which you were raised forever shapes your life. Like it or not, from the color of your eyes to the way you eat French fries, everything you are started there. You might change the way you eat French fries, but you can't change the way you were raised. For good or ill, you have to live with it. For some, separating from the family and learning to be themselves is an easier prospect than for others. In healthy families, individuals will not need to struggle to become individuals. For others, in which unhealthy emotional situations leave them damaged, there may be more of a struggle. Some will overcome the hurdles. Others will not.

Your parenting model comes from whoever raised you. Good, bad or indifferent, that's how you were imprinted. It doesn't mean it's the last word, but it is what we call your *parenting baseline*. Previous generations tended to follow a model without questioning it. Adults today are more apt to take a long look at their own upbringing to find what they liked—and what they didn't. The instant your child is born, you'll discover everybody you know is an expert on child-raising, whether they have their own children or not.

Nathaniel D. talks about a cycle that continued through his own upbringing, but one he intends to stop:

> *For years I thought my father never really loved me. He'd say he did, but it always felt like he didn't. His father had been really hard on him, but all his life he had tried to please him, and now that I'm thinking about it, I don't think he ever did. It's a hard thing to give up on, though. You always want so much to please your parents.*

I think I gave up on trying to please him much earlier in my life. It was tough. One day he'd be nice to me and I would be so happy, and the next it was back to business as usual. Eventually I just got tired of it and learned to accept him, even if I didn't respect him as much as I wish I could have. I would get so mad and say it didn't matter, I didn't care what he thought. Kids will do that out of fear and hurt, and I wasn't any different in that respect. Even at a young age, I was beginning to get a sense my father's attitude wasn't anything to do with me. My mother always reassured me of this, but it's one thing to hear it, to give lip service to it. It's another thing entirely to actually live it.

What happened to me was hard at the time, but I always thought and hoped it would end with me. I really would like to have children some day. I want to be the one to break this cycle. My father was unhappy, underneath all his anger. I hate it when I act out of anger. I work very hard to recognize that and keep it in check, to know if I'm overreacting and getting too angry. The most important thing, though, is to not treat my son, if I have one, like my father treated me. I've learned from my experience.

Favoritism is another practice that can be devastating to a child. *Daddy's little girl* is a label that can arrest emotional development. It can also wreak havoc on a male sibling, as Taylor H. describes:

My father always favored my sister. He'd often leave me out of things, or at least it felt like it. She'd get things—games and clothing—that I wouldn't. Sometimes, now that I look back on it, I realize she got things because she was with him when we'd go shopping. Instead of insisting I be there too, he'd leave me in the toy department playing and come back for me. He just didn't want to have me with him too much. I was too active, too lively. He didn't really want to be bothered. It's a lot of work being a dad. He didn't want to work hard.

My dad came from a big family and it was pretty much the same way when he grew up. The girls could do just about what ever they wanted. The boys got crushed whenever they did anything out of line. Some people learn from what happens to them, some people don't. But I can tell you this, it stops with me. When I have a family, I'll

30

remember. Girl or boy, I think I'll be a good father, but neither gets the sweet deal just because of gender. Kids deserve better than that.

Children aren't happy with nothing to ignore,
And that's what parents were created for.
—Ogden Nash

Jean F. talks about her own upbringing. She also learned how to break a cycle of some negative parenting:

My mother was left a lot in the care of her much older brother, as her own mother was a widow and the sole support of the family. So my mom grew up pretty tough. She had to be to keep up with her brother. She learned how to defend herself with humor as much as anything, and a lot of times you couldn't get very close to her—she kept her guard up with jokes. But she could turn that humor into biting sarcasm, and often did. She did the same with us kids, and lots of times it hurt pretty badly, but if you let on that it hurt, you'd be ridiculed for being "too sensitive." We learned not to be, or more realistically, not to show it. It took me years to understand I was sensitive, and it was okay. From there, I've learned how to handle my sensitivity in a positive way, to funnel it into my work and life.

I swore I'd never be as sarcastic as my mother, but sometimes I am. Can't help it sometimes, it just comes out. My mom had a pretty good B.S.-detector and she'd rip without mercy anybody who tried to pull anything on her, or in general, anybody or anything in the news she thought was bogus, we'd hear about it. I do the same with my own kids, but I've got perspective my mom didn't have, and I got it in part by finally looking at what was going on with me, and figuring out what I thought my mom had done right, and where she'd gone wrong. If they tell me they're feeling something I don't really understand, or they haven't got the words to tell me about, I'll tell them it's okay, and no, I don't quite understand, but I believe them that there's something going on. And they've learned that sense of humor, too, but they also know when I tease them, I'll stop if it gets uncomfortable. That was something my mom never did get.

My mother did the best she could. I know she loved me—loved all of us. She grew up in a time and place where survival was para-

mount. I've tried to take the best of my growing up and get rid of what didn't work and apply it to my own parenting. I learned too, you can't treat all your kids exactly the same way. It doesn't work. I guess when my kids are going through this part of their lives, they'll do what I did, and they'll do a better job than me, and so it goes. Eventually, the human race might amount to something. You don't have to blame your parents forever. You can, but you won't get any- where if you do. You'll just spin your wheels and keep on finding excuses not to succeed. I mean, it's one way to do that.

Children will live up or down to your expectations. Labeling them as incompetent or unlikely to be successful might not ensure they don't succeed, but it won't help make sure they do. At some level, at least while we're growing up, we all need and want our parents' approval. It could take a long time before we're willing to forego that approval once we know it's not likely to be granted. Children don't have the luxury of slapping a label back on parents who unfairly label them. They're stuck if you put out the message they're failures. Later on, you may be in for a payback you might not like any better than they do now.

TRY THIS

Suggest your students have a "TV-free night" with their families. Discuss the benefits of giving up television. Brainstorm a list of activities to take the place of TV time together. Be imaginative. Conduct a survey to see how many families are willing to give it a try.

A minister once visited a prison to speak to a large group of in- mates. He asked how many of them were told when they were children they would end up in jail. The minister was shocked when almost ev- eryone present raised their hand. Parents need to believe in their children and predict a good future for them.

Instead try saying, "You're going through some hard times right now, but I want you to know I'll never give up on you."

When our first child was growing into the toddler phase and her command of language was increasing, I became more concerned than ever that her father only seemed to praise her for being pretty. I really had to work hard to make sure I praised her for any other accomplishment. It made it a lopsided deal, but it was the best I could do. He simply did not understand, and would not recognize, how important it was to start early reinforcing concepts other than the physical.

—Abby F.

Did you ever hear either of these? "You'll never amount to anything," or "You want to be *what*? You're not smart enough to do that."

At one point when I was growing up, I thought about becoming a doctor. My father, in typical style, let me know just what he thought of me. He told me quite plainly I was not smart enough and I'd never make it. It was enough to discourage me. Later I developed a passion for writing. He was just as positive about that. This time I was a few years older and a few years more determined. I didn't let him get in my way. My mother was always encouraging. Whether she really liked what I wrote or not, I don't know, but she always knew what to say. She told me I could be a writer. I told myself that, too. Giving myself that name went a long way to establishing an identity as a writer. That's why I'm convinced parents can go a long way down either road to helping or hurting their kids make the most of themselves. The right word can send them down the right road.

—Mark W.

TRY THIS

Message in a bottle: Is there something you'd like to share with your family, maybe something they don't know about you? Gather a stock of empty containers—yes, even margarine tubs, as long as they have lids. Then, visit your local discount store for wrapping paper if your containers are to be gifts. Have students write their secret message on a piece of paper and decorate it. Enclose it in the container and wrap the gift.

Variation: Write secret messages and wrap them as described above, but have a gift exchange in the classroom. The teacher can distribute the gifts and each student guesses to see if they know whose secret message it was.

Finding ways to help your children grow and develop their independence can often be very simple. Look for opportunities.

When we went grocery shopping, once they were older, I would assign both of my kids a mission. We made it into a game. One was sent to find bread, another to find spaghetti, for example. Some items they knew where to find. They were always tickled to find something and bring it back. Not only had they accomplished their mission, but they were able to help. It's hard to overestimate how big an ego boost that is for a kid. Some items they couldn't find, but that was okay, too. I would praise them for their hard work in searching for it, and then we'd track it down together. Besides, you never succeed at everything, whether you're a kid or an adult. Handling small failures in a positive way might just teach them how to deal with the bigger ones.

—Nora L.

When children are very young, their parents are their whole world. A harsh word from a parent and a lot more than a child's day can be ruined. What we say is gospel, and if what we say is negative and labeling, we can send a shock wave into the soul that may not die for a long time, if ever. Were you ever told to think before you speak? Did you so completely learn that lesson that you've never done the same to your own kids? Most of us can think of at least one time we've let fly with words that smacked a hard blow. We'd give anything to drag out the old fishing pole and reel those words back in, but it's too late. That's why labeling by a parent is so powerful. The labels limit us while we're growing up, and if we take them with us into adult life, they can limit there, too.

TRY THIS

For adults: Let yourself off the hook. Think of one time you spoke quickly in anger, without thinking, and hurt a child. Forgive yourself. If you could take back the words, what would you say instead?

As Pam discovered, *how* we say anything to a child may be even more important than *what* we say:

Sarcastic? Ooh, you never met a woman as sarcastic as my mother! She would say stuff that would filet you like a haddock, no lie. Then, if your feelings were hurt, she'd tell you not to be a baby, it was just a joke. But she never knew when to stop. She hurt my feelings a lot, let me tell you. I'm sarcastic with my own kids, but they definitely know it's humor, and it's mostly not aimed at them. I rarely lose control like that. I'm funny, anyway, and sarcasm is just the way I juggle words in clever ways. I've told them to watch the way they speak and to whom. I've tried to teach them who they can joke around with in this way, and who they can't. If someone is really sensitive and can't handle jokes like that, it's not worth it to be that way.

Parents of my generation are extremely conscious about what it means to "model behavior." My parents thought it an affront if anybody besides Dr. Spock offered advice on child raising. On the other hand, there's me and my generation. I know I am much more aware of the "don't do as I do, do as I say" school of parenting, and I know that is not the way to raise kids. You can see one hundred things and do one just once and they'll, sure as God made little green apples, copy what you did instead of what you said. All the way down the line.

When we were all grown we were pretty much scattered all across the country, but when we did get together, we'd have the inevitable mother bashing session. It sounds mean spirited, but looking back on it, it was therapeutic. We took care of some long-standing resentments, even between ourselves. Sort of like in one of those cathartic homecoming movies, except we never did it with our mother involved. She wouldn't have participated in anything like that. She'd been born to be reticent about feelings. But us, one of those sessions could last for hours.

One of my sisters told us some of the names our mother had called her. It shocked me. She carried those for a long time before she forgave our mother.

—Pam T.

Govern a family as you would cook a small fish—very gently.
—Chinese proverb

Kids can become an extension of parents' inabilities. Without awareness, it's easy to live through our kids, to have them compensate us for the gaps in our own childhood. John H., father of two, relates his story:

My father was pretty hard on me and my brothers and sisters. I spent a good portion of my growing up years working in his business, and missing out on things I really wanted to do, especially sports. I guess some part of me never really dealt with that, never forgave him. He was tough on us boys, but the girls were more or less off the hook. Now my own son tells me he thinks I'm much tougher on him than I am on his sister, and the only time he really feels like I love him is when he does well in sports, no matter what other things he does well. At first, I got pretty mad. It's not easy hearing something like that from your kid, even if he is all grown up now. Our relationship isn't too good. I don't think he's right, but I don't know. Maybe.

One, Two, Three—Birth Order Labeling

One of the most obvious types of labeling within the family is by birth order. Did you ever feel like you were only a number? It may have started with your family.

I was the oldest of five, and boy, did I fit the stereotype of the oldest child in that I was ultra-responsible. My parents gave me lots of responsibility and the labels that go with looking after the young ones—and doing it so well. The thing is I can't get mad at them for that. They were really proud of me for being a straight arrow, and somebody they could depend on. I learned very young to look after kids, earn money babysitting and stuff, and I know they meant well. It's just funny years later, when everybody else had outgrown their rebellious streak 'cause they'd done it when they were teenagers, that's when I found time to rebel. I guess by then I had figured out being responsible 24/7 could get on a person's nerves. It never gave them time to find out what else they could be. I had never figured out what else I could be. It was time. High time.

—Brad M.

Scientists who study human behavior, some more than others, are firm believers in the significance of birth order. Advocates of this belief find it an overall determining factor in how we grow up. Others say research lacks scientific proof of its importance. *Science* magazine featured a special report by John Tierney on "The Myth of the Firstborn."

Tierney says "Birth order theory makes an appealing, neat way to categorize human beings—like astrology but with scientific trappings."

TRY THIS

Gather data about the number of single children and those who have siblings. Make charts and graphs with the data. Just gathering the data will generate discussion. Share your birth order with the group. Talk about how it has affected your life.

As the oldest of five, I always had a lot of responsibility. That was something I assumed naturally when I was a kid. That's what I had to do, so that's what I did. It didn't really bother me until later. Somewhere along the line I acquired the idea I'd be responsible for the rest of them forever. I took it for granted, without being aware of it, I would take the lead and the responsibility in just about any given situation. It never occurred to me it would be otherwise. I was always "our responsible oldest, who helps take care of all her brothers and sisters."

Many years later, my mother died. She hadn't been really healthy for many years, but her death came suddenly and unexpectedly. I had one sibling in town and the other two flew in from out of town. Imagine my shock, when, before I knew it, everything was organized, handled, taken care of. One of my siblings had always been a bit bossy, but now she was in middle management of a large company back east. She took over. I figured it was her way of dealing with grief—keeping busy. I didn't say anything, but I still sit back and marvel at just how much the roles of our childhood had gone by the wayside. When we were growing up, she was "the baby" and I was "our grown-up one." In one click I had been relegated from being in charge to being told. It took me a while to come to terms with a different view of myself in the world.

It still feels a bit weird and disorienting. You get so much of your view of your image from your place in the family. And yes, I know once you're out in the world any ideas you had based on that image may change, but somehow it hadn't occurred to me my family was part of the world. We were self-contained in that respect. That's how my ego had interpreted it anyway. It doesn't always work out that way.

—Eliza F.

Make a family tree. Have students bring in photos (or color copies so as not to destroy original photos) and other family memorabilia. Some students will have access to more of this than others. Make magazines and newspapers available for those who can't bring in photos. Use cutouts or draw portraits to represent missing or unavailable photos.

Talk about birth order. Discuss how it affects the student's position in the family, what they're expected to do, etc. Would they like to change their position in the family? Why? Don't forget to see if there are any singles in the group. "Only children" occupy their own special niche. Some students may envy that position. Singles may like it because they're the only child who needs attention. They may dislike it because they would like to have siblings. Be sure to emphasize the point is to discuss how different types of families affect who we are, and all kinds of families are just fine.

Regardless of *how* significant it is, it is significant. Like other aspects of our lives, some of its importance will come down to how much we *let* it be important. That's when we're adults, of course. By then we've had time to assess the way we were raised. We can look at our family structure and our place in it. Just as the river is never the same river the second time you dip your toe into it, the family is never the same family after subsequent children are born. Life changes all the time. Birth order is a significant factor in the family dynamic.

I read first-born children tend to be more the placatory types. This is true for me. They're also supposed to have the most self-esteem of the siblings. This is not true of me. I was so conciliatory people would walk all over me all the time. I used to complain about it and my siblings would get all over my case. That was annoying, but then, it always is when somebody's right about something you're screwing up. Of course they didn't have any particular insights as to how to help me learn to stop doing what I was doing. I had to figure that out for myself. We all have to, right? It sure would have helped if somebody could just have said something without pointing the finger and blaming me.

It's a funny thing, being the oldest. I just don't fit the mold of the first-born very much, except for years and years I felt an obligation to be the "team leader." I felt obligated to keep in touch with everybody, make sure everybody else kept in touch, stuff like that. I finally got the message I wasn't needed in that role anymore. Why not step back? We're all grown up now. I don't need to look after them any more.

—Fern G.

Who are you like? Are you tall and fair like Aunt Marcia? Are you a fighter like Uncle Joe? Labeling behaviors as something a child does because he was "born that way" makes it easy to dismiss the behavior as something beyond anyone's control. It makes it much more difficult for the parent to change their thinking about the child, or set limits and help the child learn better ways to act, even if that's what's needed.

The Beat Doesn't Have to Go On

Children have a birth order, but they don't need to *be* it. Surveys show parents tend to find ways their kids live up to labels. The stereotypes may be true in your family. Stereotypes arise from common truths, but it doesn't mean you have to yield to them or describe your kids that way. If you have three children, the middle child can be referred to as "John's brother." It might sound or feel awkward, but change has that effect at first.

Common sense goes a long way. If you have an athletic, shy or outgoing child, others will know this by observing your youngster. Children certainly know it. By assigning them this label, you may be setting some behaviors in stone in the child's mind. You can cut down on sibling rivalry very easily by recognizing each child for individual accomplishments. Encourage each to develop their own interests. Rather than labeling a child as clumsy, find a strength and recognize it.

Try not to label kids by their personality types. Were you known as the shy one? Identifying a shy child or a bold child in this fashion, you may well help the child ingrain that trait. Spending regular time with children individually will help establish and maintain their separate personalities. It will help parents get to know their kids in a way that strengthens their separate bonds. Encourage separate activities for each child to enhance their own abilities. Does this mean you should not allow them to engage in the same things? Not at all. Often family members will share interests in sports, music or both. Not only is this a pursuit for the individual, but for the family as well.

TRY THIS

For parents: Challenge your children by finding something for them to do that runs contrary to the dominant strain of their personality. A little gentle role-switching can help everyone grow. The child who's always neat and orderly doesn't have to be the one you ask for help in putting away the groceries, for example. And your child who's always so full of energy can enjoy a quiet moment reading to a younger sibling or helping you put the groceries away. For teachers, the same type of role-switching can work in a classroom.

Some traditions belong in the past. If you feel your parents' child-raising style needs revision, do it. Every generation can strive to do a better job in raising the next. It's no longer necessary for anyone to try and go it alone if there are problems in the family. Resources are available for families of all income levels. With an increase in population, crime, and drug use, many of us have become distrustful and suspicious of our neighbors. It might seem like the old-fashioned spirit of neighborhood and community has disappeared, the spirit that functioned as a support system for many.

I'm really proud of myself for getting past what I was taught with regard to emotional problems. I was taught anything like that stayed in the family. You didn't discuss it with other people. I learned to seek help, or just talk to friends. I don't try to handle everything alone anymore. It's a big relief.

—Marie H.

TRY THIS

Organize a block party, either around a holiday or just because. If you're naturally shy, this is a good opportunity to step outside your comfort zone. If you have children, take them with you as you canvas your block or your building to drum up interest. A *just because* party can have a theme like "Let's Get Acquainted," which will help everybody pull together on a united front. Don't be discouraged. Even if only one other family joins you, there
(continued)

will be two families united. And if you hadn't known each other before, you do now. Try it again a few months later. This time the other family (or families) can join you to round up participants.

Variations: Organize neighbors for a child-care exchange. If it doesn't serve well for work times, arrange it so parents can get some time away evenings, or for shopping, or whatever works for you. Think of as many ways you can to help each other out. Make it a "Lean On Me" exchange. Perhaps an older person could use a ride to the grocery store or pharmacy, or just might like some company.

Parenting Styles

Most authorities recognize three main styles of parenting: authoritarian, permissive, and assertive-democratic. Do you know your parenting style?

TRY THIS

Before you read any further, decide which is your style by name alone. Compare your decision with what you find out after reading the descriptions.

Are you an authoritarian parent? This parent values obedience above all else. The child is told what to do and what not to do. Rules are clear and unbending. The parent pours the right information into the child who is considered an empty vessel. Misbehavior is strictly punished. Although this was predominant for most of Western history, authoritarian parenting is mainly effective in societies experiencing little change. They are usually accepting of just one way to do things, for example in agrarian-industrial societies. A "master teacher" (often the parent) instructs the child on each act (such as sowing the seeds and weeding the fields). The child learns by imitating the expert.

This style mismatches a rapidly changing society that values choice and innovation. Rebellion often results from strict punishment, including spanking. Spanking, which models violence as a solution to problems, doesn't work in a society that claims to value peaceful solutions. Children raised to follow the "expert" easily copy anyone, including undesirable peers. Clipping their wings, so to speak, doesn't allow for them to grow to learn good judgment.

Are you a permissive parent? This style was popular in the 1950s and 1960s. It was a reaction to the horrors of whole nations mindlessly following dictators of World War II. Instead of following, children are encouraged to think for themselves, avoid inhibitions, and not value conformity. Parents take a "hands-off" approach, allowing children to learn from the consequences of their actions. Misbehavior is usually ignored.

Although those raised in this style are creative and original, they often have trouble living in a highly populated community, as well as fitting into the workforce. Ignoring misbehavior gives no information about expected behavior. With no intervention, the bully wins, and the passive child loses—a perfect setup to be a victim later in life. Victims take no responsibility for their behavior, either successes or failures, and bullies suffer no penalties. Aggressive patterns become ingrained when children are not guided to find acceptable ways to get their desires met.

This style had some hope of success in the child-oriented fifties and sixties. Usually one consistent adult was available to patiently guide self-discovery to the consequences of actions. Today's society is fast-paced. It's often the village raising the child, with a multitude of adults playing into the child's life each week. Without clear limits, children get confused, feel insecure, and can make poor choices.

Are you an assertive-democratic parent? These parents establish basic guidelines for children. They clarify issues, they give reasons for limits. Learning to take responsibility is a high priority. Children are given lots of practice in making choices and guided to see the consequences of those choices. Misbehavior is handled with an appropriate consequence, or by problem-solving with the child, to find an acceptable way to get his or her desires met. Out-of-control children have "time out", not punishment. Children are part of deciding how to make amends when someone or something has been hurt. They're asked to put themselves into the wronged child's place. Assertive-democratic parenting works for today's fast-changing information age where choice is constant and there is no longer just one "right" way. Children raised by this style learn to accept responsibility, make wiser choices, and cope with change. In general, they're better equipped to succeed in a workforce that relies on cooperative problem solving.

Most authorities agree a blend of the three styles is the most effective.

EYE OPENER

Take a moment to assess your style. Is it working for you and your child(ren)? Is it the same as, or different from, the style in which you were raised? Teachers function *in loco parentis*, or as parents, in the classroom. Is your teaching style the same as your parenting style?

TRY THIS

About My Family: Have students work with a partner. Younger students may need an adult helper. The partners should interview each other using the questions below (or tailor the questions to your class).

1. An important thing to know about my family is _____ .
2. I'm proud of my family because _____ .
3. Other people like my family because_____ .
4. The best thing about my family is _____ .
5. If a new friend came to visit, the first thing I would show him or her about my family is _____ .
6. I like my family because _____ .
7. My family has the most fun together when we_____ .

After these questions are answered, each partner should ask the other "What is the most important thing you learned about your partner's family?" Share the results with the class. Discuss how families are the same, and how they are different.

Some families face the challenge of one or more children being labeled *exceptional.* This label applies to those with special problems related to physical disabilities, sensory impairments, emotional disturbances, learning disabilities, and mental retardation. Most of these children require a great deal of understanding and patience, not to mention special education and services. This undeniably alters the family dynamic. Just how much and in what manner is up to the parents, and the level of support they're getting from the community and other family members. It also calls into question, again, a label we all toss around: normal.

When my second child was born, I knew something was wrong. There was something different about her right from the beginning.

They told me, after a while, she had Down's Syndrome. It was a bit of a shock, I'll admit, because you just don't expect it. Then it was time to just get busy and take care of her. I know my husband and other child felt like they were left on their own a lot. I couldn't help it. I did the best I could, it's just that she had so many health problems right away, like most Down's kids.

I never got bothered when people called her retarded. She was retarded. It's not shameful to be retarded. It bothered me when people would stare at her when I took her to the doctor or out to eat at McDonald's. I remember a few years ago my other daughter heaving a big sigh and saying she wished, just once, that her sister was "normal." As she said it, I felt angry. Very angry. But I took a step back and calmed down, and I just gave her a big hug. We'd already had, by that time, too many conversations about what a "special" kid her sister was, and mostly she was extremely helpful and sweet. When you're a kid, though, it can be tough when people are giving your sister funny looks, like she's some kind of freak or something.

—Renee G.

Parents of exceptional children (the term used in education) must themselves be educated to the use of the label *exceptional.* Parents of children with learning disabilities can require some counseling as to how to explain these circumstances to their children. One counselor described a child who came to her office in tears, saying she had half a brain and she would never be able to learn. In reality, the girl was dyslexic and had been given the label *half-brained* by a well-meaning parent trying to spare her daughter the pain of being called dummy, or worse, by her peers. Many parents find the label *learning disabled* shameful. More are worried that their children will find their self-image shattered, or they will feel inferior or different.

TRY THIS

Where *do* labels belong? Have students suggest the kinds of things that should be labeled, like food. Younger students can incorporate spelling words by drawing labels for the cans and jars. Design posters using catchy phrases, like "Label Beans, Not People!" Older students can work in groups and come up with advertising campaigns using this strategy to help educate their peers about the dangers of labeling people.

How can parents and children deal with labels in the family? One way is to play. Play is crucial to growing up and is based on specific skills. In play, the child learns to deal with the adult world by mimicking it. In play, children express their emotions. They also learn how to put the brakes on their impulsiveness. They learn to adjust their behavior and emotions as called for by the rules of social settings. Play helps children develop good social skills. Research consistently points to developing solid friendships early in life as a way to increasing self-esteem and good mental health. In learning all these skills through play, children can acquire the ability to deal with others in a constructive fashion.

TRY THIS

Spend some time observing children at play. Make a note of the types of interactions taking place. During the time you observe, are any labels emerging? How do the children handle them? Create stories appropriate for the age groups of the children, in which the characters find positive ways to interact with each other. If you observe play in which children are echoing the types of behaviors you're trying to impart, craft a story to reinforce those ideas. Although there is an abundance of quality literature, it's important to realize as educators and parents we can also write stories as fun teaching tools. Students respond enthusiastically to teacher-created material.

EYE OPENER

When was the last time you played? Adults can easily lose the childlike side of their personalities. Do you play with your children or do you just watch them? What can you do in your life to enjoy some playfulness?

TRY THIS

For adults: Keep a small bottle of bubbles in your car. The next time you get stuck in rush hour traffic, open the window, open the bubbles, and blow a few into the air. You might feel silly. You might also get a good laugh and relieve some stress. You might inspire someone around you to try the same thing. Just don't forget to keep your eyes on the traffic!

Children learn the positive values of treating each other with respect and taking responsibility for their own behavior. The steps to teaching social skills are similar to teaching academic subjects, except that play, group activities and discussion play stronger roles. Identify the skill that needs to be learned. Younger children particularly enjoy the use of puppets and dolls to tell stories. Storytelling is a highly effec-tive tool. Always be on the lookout for that teachable moment. Provide opportunities for students to reinforce what they learn. Have the sto-ries acted out for the class. When possible, invite other classes and even parents.

Children who talk about their feelings are less likely to turn to alcohol or drugs or join gangs. Some of the skills that can be taught and reinforced are eye contact, smiling, taking turns, listening to others, inhibiting behaviors that threaten others, following directions, shar-ing uncomfortable feelings, stopping sarcasm, and egging others on. Of course the teacher will always need to keep cultural differences in mind as well, since some cultures regard direct eye contact as a threat. En-courage the use of "I" sentences, such as, "I like it when you ask me what I'd like to play," or "I feel hurt when you tease me." Even very young children can model this type of behavior.

Encourage children to use their natural strengths to help others as well as themselves. Sharing the most important resources—them-selves—goes a long way toward developing friendships and unity between individual students and within a classroom.

I remember one boy in particular from my first year of teaching. He was struggling at the beginning of the school year because English was not his first language. Even so, you could tell this boy was a natural born leader. The other kids would follow his lead even though they literally didn't always understand what he was saying. Because he was having a hard time, he'd act out when, ordinarily, I don't think he would have. I came up with a strategy that took care of both problems at once. I enlisted the help of his classmates in teaching him English.

It was kindergarten, and children at that age truly love to help. My student was eager to learn. We all had a great time. No matter where he went in the classroom or what he did or touched or used, somebody was there to give him the English word for it. He loved it, we loved it. By the end of the year, he was fluent in English. Not only that, but he had become a very effective classroom leader and helper. He was a strong-willed child, but one you could appeal to by address-ing his sense of justice and fair play, and one who had the potential to be an effective leader as an adult, because he listened as well as acted.

I learned a great deal from working with him, and from enlisting the other children, too. At the beginning of the year, when this boy first joined the class, there were a lot of misunderstood feelings all around. The other children resented this boy's bullying of them, and he was fearful and acting out accordingly. They learned, by working together, to trust each other. They all learned to better deal with their feelings, too, since this was something we talked about a good deal.

—Violet F.

Some higher level social skills are resolving conflict, listening with empathy when pain and hurt are described, giving support and encouragement and creative problem solving. Social skills training gives children a bigger bag of tricks from which to choose. Children can learn techniques to deal with threat and their anger. The habitually angry child can learn hostility and threat are not always present just because he thinks they are.

TRY THIS

Do you have a child who constantly struggles with controlling anger? Individual behavior contracts have been in the teacher's toolbox for many years. They're still a good idea in some circumstances. If one child needs particular help, utilize your school's resources to do so. Another simple but effective technique is to slow down the breathing. The first step is for the child to recognize when they're in danger of losing their temper. This may be the hard part of the equation. Once that's accomplished, have the student learn to take a very long, slow breath through the nose, hold for a count of five, and then let it out very slowly through the mouth, also to a count of five. Vary the technique as needed. Do it with your student. He or she may be skeptical. Use the technique yourself as a way of dealing with stress, in the classroom and out. Assure your student you've used this tool and found it helpful.

Variations: The whole class can find anger management tools helpful. Try a "give yourself a hug" moment. This is more likely to succeed with younger children than older students. As a way of diverting angry thinking, have students recite newly learned information like math facts or days of the week.

Anger is a normal human emotion, even in families. Parents get angry, too. They can say things in anger they wish they hadn't said.

Everybody has done something silly, thoughtless or embarrassing. Do we want those things pointed out to us? Why do we often feel free to say things in the context of the family we would never say in other company? Imagine you just tripped coming up the steps. Your spouse observes. He or she helps you up, sarcastically saying, "Very graceful." You feel dumb and the sarcasm is unwelcome, but you cope with it. Perhaps they say it in a light-hearted tone, and perhaps you're ready to laugh at yourself. What if you're not? What if you've had a rough day and this is the last straw?

What if it were your child in that situation? Did anything like that happen to you when you were a child? You'd be the exception if you said no. Did you hear "clumsy" thrown out in that circumstance? Chances are, somewhere along the line, you did. We need not raise a generation of people unable to laugh at themselves but we can try raising a generation who think of compassionate reactions before hurtful ones. Many challenges in family life, however, are not solved with understanding alone. We also need to set limits and do problem solving. As you get better and better at showing compassionate understanding with your children, they will feel more loved and more confident in their ability to solve problems. And they will feel more love and trust with you.

As the National Committee for Prevention of Child Abuse says, "Take time out. Don't take it out on your kid!" Know it's okay to be angry. Involve everyone in managing stress and anger in ways that benefit the family. Make sure your child realizes you are reaching out for help in anger reduction, not calling someone to blame him or her. By-pass a negative anger reaction by going directly into problem solving. Don't try to place blame. Determine what is needed to correct the situation. Also try:
- taking a warm bath
- smelling a flower
- petting an animal
- hugging a teddy bear
- calling Parents Anonymous or a sympathetic friend
- making a cup of tea or drinking a glass of water

Two of the most solid things to remember when dealing with children are that children are not little adults, and you should punish the behavior, not the child. These are true for teens as well as younger children.

Chapter Three

Me, Myself, and I

---

*"The world is made for people who aren't
cursed with self-awareness."*

—the character Annie Savoy
in the film *Bull Durham*

Self respect—the secure feeling that no one, as yet, is suspicious.
—H. L. Mencken

---

*Do I contradict myself? Very well then I contradict myself.
(I am large, I contain multitudes.)*
—Walt Whitman

The Fox and the Mask

Somehow or other, a Fox got into the storeroom of a theater.
Suddenly he observed a face glaring down on him and began to be
very frightened. Looking more closely, he found it was only a Mask
such as actors use to put over their face. "Ah," said the Fox, "you
look very fine. It's a pity you have no brains."

Outside show is a poor substitute for inner worth.

EYE OPENER

Someone has just asked you to describe yourself in one word. What is your
response?

It might seem contradictory to the aims of this book to ask that question, but sufficient self-knowledge helps us describe who we are. Although labels put things in boxes, they can also be a quick assessment of just where we are. Do you like the label you gave yourself? Was it fair? Was it accurate? Is it something you can live with if you were never asked that question again? What was your reaction to just being asked? Did you say, "That's not fair! I'm more than one thing!" If the label says *corn* that's what's in the can. People aren't quite as limited. Or rather, they don't need to be.

My parents were born during the depression. It was a time for being practical. By that I mean for most working class folks there wasn't time or sympathy for looking inwards. You just got out there and took care of things. When I got to an age where I was starting to look critically at the world around me, to do some real thinking about things, including myself, my world, my place in it, all I heard was about "kooks" who indulged in introspection. Introspection was almost swearing in our house.

I know better now. Once I wasn't in the house any more, there was no stony look to silence the thoughts. It took a long time before I figured some things out, and came to realize my self-analysis was healthy and not self-indulgent. Actually, by the time I went to see a therapist, I had sort of evolved into the need for trying to fix what was wrong without worrying too much about why they had gone wrong.

—Amelia W.

EYE OPENER

Think of some other labels for yourself. What can you add to the one-word description you came up with at the beginning of this chapter?

Over the last hundred years, the concept of self-esteem has grown. It began as a fragile idea used to ground the newly emerging discipline of psychology. It's now regarded as a basic truth about human experience and motivation. Self-esteem has become one of the more important and prolific concepts in psychological research, psychotherapy, and popular discussions of the self and self-help. What started as something so small has become not only the foundation of much of psychology but also a billion dollar industry.

EYE OPENER

What one word would your best friend use to describe you? What word would you use to describe your friend?

It's not surprising that high levels of self-esteem lead to a host of positive attributes, such as good academic performance, well-adjusted children, happy marriages, and a healthy sex life. Low levels of self-esteem, on the other hand, have been linked to such widely varying issues and problems as teenage pregnancy, suicide, fire starting, and homicide.

TRY THIS

Me Cake: Cakes have many ingredients. What goes into the cake that makes you? Have children write the recipe that makes them who they are. List the ingredients that make you as an example. One child might be a half-cup of sports, two cups of music, a pinch of grandparents, two table-spoons family, and a sprinkling of friends. Bake for (insert age of child) years and voila! The recipes can be illustrated and displayed around the classroom.

By nurture or nature, we learn the art of labeling. That includes labeling ourselves.

I was pretty young when it was discovered I had some musical talent. The only reason anybody found out was because the teacher put me in the choir, as she said, to give me some place where I could use my mouth without getting into trouble. Nobody knew, until then, I could sing.

This tickled my mother to no end. Nobody else in the family showed the slightest inclination to music, and nobody in her family ever had. She loved to sing, but seldom did, as she was undoubtedly a very bad singer. So I found myself going to a music teacher for singing lessons. I really wanted to play the violin, but my parents were not prepared to accept the awful stuff that comes out of a beginning strings player. I can't fault them too much for that!

My mother also, once she discovered this vein of music in me, would sit me down on those weekends when Leonard Bernstein would be on TV with his concerts for young people. To be honest, at the time I could have cared less about classical music, but I was no slouch. This got me attention—very positive attention, and not just for good grades or for helping out with my younger siblings, but genuine praise. I remember enough to know it felt like no other attention I ever received from my parents. It definitely set me aside from the pack and labeled me as "the musical one."

The irony is, to this day, I still am the only one of the five of us with any musical talent. By telling myself at the time I was musical (even though I didn't understand what that was all about), I ultimately became very musical and went on to study music at college. I have passed my musical ability to my own children, both of whom feel that genuine love of music and cherish it as part of their lives as I do.

I wish I hadn't accepted some of the other labels so fully as I did. My parents also labeled me the "responsible one," the "good student," and things like that. I know people have been called horrendous things, things that scarred them permanently. I'm not saying that's what happened to me. What the labels did for me was solidify my self-conception that getting good grades was who and what I was, and that was about it. They didn't do anything wrong. In their own way they were singing my praises, but they didn't believe in the idea of introspection, and what it did was put me in a very strict box with small dimensions. It took me years to learn I was more than the sum of several report cards.

Eventually, I had to cast off some of the behaviors that went with the labels, if only to examine what the labels really meant. For example, when I got to the last few years of college, I stopped worrying so much about getting the grades and started getting more involved with other activities. I didn't totally abandon the label behavior. If you've done something long enough, it becomes part of who you are. If you've had a label attached to you and you figure out—usually after a lot of heartache and bad times—it isn't part of you, then you can learn to let go of it, and stop doing whatever it is that makes the label true.

—Anne F.

Me, Myself, and I

The modern fable of *King Leo*, by Fay Farquhar, emphasizes the need for self-knowledge:

A long time ago, when kings and queens were commonplace and so were stories like this, there was a king whose name was Leo. He had reigned for many years in a land of forests and beautiful water and rich, fertile farmland. For all those many years the people had worked hard and been prosperous. Leo was a good man and a good king. Things were going well. People had jobs and enough to eat. Crime was not much in evidence.

As always happens, though, their grumbling started as a little noise. The little noise grew into a big noise. But noises are sometimes like sneezes or yawns—they're catching.

"King Leo is a bad king," said one. "King Leo is not regal enough," said another. "What does regal mean?" asked another. "Well I'm not quite sure," replied the person who had complained, "but I know it's something a king is supposed to be."

Word soon came to him the people were very discontented.

"I must be a bad king," Leo said to himself. He called his advisors to assist him in his search for a way to fix the problems. The first advisor suggested the king grow a beard. All regal monarchs have beards."

King Leo had his doubts, but agreed. Soon he had a fine full beard streaked with gray, as was his hair. It didn't help. The grumbling continued. Again he summoned the council.

"The beard has changed nothing," he told the councilor who suggested it.

"Although it does indeed look distinguished, your Highness," added another.

"Perhaps your Majesty could shave it off," another councilor suggested. King Leo shook his head for again he had his doubts, but complied with the suggestion. Again, it didn't help. The grumbling in the kingdom was growing louder.

"Perhaps your Majesty should let his royal hair grow long," came the suggestion. "In the old days of the kingdom it was the custom." Growing a beard hadn't helped but after all these were his councilors, the wisest men and women in the kingdom. So he took their advice and grew his hair. It didn't help.

At the next meeting he was offered: "Perhaps short hair is the answer, Majesty."

The king sighed, but he cut his hair very short. It didn't help.

"I am an incompetent king," he said. "I have failed to quiet the unhappiness."

Another of his councilors said, "It was also the custom in the olden days for kings to wear long royal robes trimmed in ermine fur. Your Majesty might consider that."

So King Leo ordered a robe to be made, except he asked that no real fur be used. Even fake fur did not help this suggestion work. The grumbling was growing.

One more suggestion was made. "Perhaps your Majesty should go jump in the lake—to take a swim."

The king did this. It did not fix the problem. After a month of swimming daily the king still had not noticed any improvement, except in his cardiovascular system. One day after his swim he sat by the side of the lake and spoke out loud even though there was nobody around to listen except the ducks.

"First I grew a beard then shaved it off, then I grew my hair then cut it off. Then I had a new royal robe made and now I've been swimming and nothing seems to work. The people are still unhappy. Now what shall I do? What shall I do?"

He paced up and down along the lake. He paced from early in the morning until the shadows fell from the setting sun, even waving off his attendants who had come with food. He watched as a mother bird patiently taught her babies to fly. Over and over she showed them and over and over they tried. At last the solution came to him.

"That's it!" he said finally. I just had to be myself and trust myself. How foolish I was to call myself a bad king." So he let his hair grow back to the medium way it had been before, and grew a mustache, which he had not had before but everybody needs a change now and then, gave the robe to the children's theater so they could make it into a curtain for the puppet theater.

King Leo continued his swimming because it was good exercise and he enjoyed it but he did not expect it to solve any other problems. Instead he found out exactly who it was who was complaining. He discovered they were people who just liked complaining and grumbling because they just weren't going to be happy no matter what and *there was not a thing anybody could do to make them happy. They were given jobs to do around the kingdom, cleaning the sides of the road, repairing public facilities and other types of public service work. At the end of the day they were much too tired to complain. Besides, it finally dawned on them they could get together and fix just about anything if they tackled it the right way.*

King Leo had lots of help, but it in the end, no matter what people called him; he had to figure out who he really was.

TO THINK ABOUT

Are there things about yourself you would like to change? Is this a result of something somebody has said about you or something you've decided on your own? What is your plan to make the changes? Is it realistic?

We learn at a young age what labels people are willing to accept about us.

I learned very early I was awkward. How did I learn that? Simple. My parents let me know with their teasing and jokes about my lack of physical prowess, jokes that went too far. I wasn't supposed to let on if my feelings were hurt. Though I was praised often for my academic capabilities, it was the razzing about what I couldn't do that registered more with me. You know the old story—do ninety-nine things right and one wrong, and the one wrong thing is the one you'll hear about. The way it worked with me is I seemed to hear that one thing the loudest. Growing up when I did, though, you never said much back to your parents. I don't think that was just me.

—Elsie M.

We create our self-image over a lifetime, sometimes exacting standards of performance from ourselves that give rise to perfectionism. It also helps avoid the hurt of rejection as well as other negative aspects of life. Because *you* created that self-image, *you* can reevaluate yourself as an adult, with adult standards, and create a positive self-image. Self-esteem is a blend of internal confidence, external achievements, and compassion for yourself. Compassion allows you to forgive your mistakes and preserve your self-esteem. Compassion also allows you to put unreasonable values and rules in perspective.

There is a difference between self-esteem and self-concept, but neither is inborn. Self-concept is learned. As far as we know, no one is born with a self-concept. It gradually emerges in the early months of life. It's shaped and reshaped through repeated perceived experiences, particularly with significant others. We're all works in progress. Basic perceptions of ourselves are quite stable, so change takes time. Rome was not built in a day, and neither is self-concept or self-esteem. We are all born, however, with personalities that render us different right off the bat.

Until my second child was born, I had no strong ideas about babies having different personalities, but believe me, they do! My first child was what most people call an easy baby, meaning she seldom fussed, was easy to soothe, and a very calm child. My second was the complete opposite. He was what was labeled colicky—often difficult to soothe and needed much more attention than his sister. He didn't handle any kind of separation easily. He's not like that now that he's a teenager, but the basic difference in temperament remains. The first is, for the most part, even-tempered, and the other more volatile. At this age I might have anticipated differences, not as infants. Of course it's of no use at all to label babies, especially for first-time parents. Labels can really rattle them. It can make them doubt themselves as parents, and for something that's just the nature of the child.

—Laura. R.

TO THINK ABOUT

Mario Puzo sent *The Godfather* to seventeen publishers before it was accepted.

TRY THIS

For adults and older learners: Use the above as a springboard for a discussion about failure. Failure can be used as a label, but a failure in our lives can also be the turning of a closed door down one alleyway into an open door at the end of the next.

For younger children: Very young children also need to begin to deal with failure. Small hands often don't succeed the first time they attempt tasks. Children, depending on their nature, will either accept this or not. What works with one child may not work with another, but patience is seldom wasted. Share a story of something you had a hard time mastering.

EYE OPENER

What was something important you tried that didn't succeed right away? How did you react? Did anyone tell you that you couldn't succeed? Did that influence you? If you were to try the same project again, how would you approach it differently?

Because self-concept is largely developed through experience, there's ample opportunity for growth and change. It's a two-edged sword, however. The way we perceive ourselves is often different than how others perceive us. We see ourselves at different times with varying degrees of clarity. It is important to be able to look inward. It's not quite this fragile, but visualize yourself walking a tightrope. You've got two safety nets. On one side is your own self-image, on the other are peoples' perceptions of you. The tightrope is in the middle. It's closest to the *real* you.

TRY THIS

If possible, obtain a fun house mirror and have the children look at themselves. If not, obtain pictures of an image in such a mirror, or section off pieces of the mirror with masking tape. Do something to alter the mirror so perceptions are altered. Have kids look at themselves in a distorted, but funny, way. Have them draw the image. Even those kids who feel they can't draw will be successful because the images are so out of proportion. Use the distorted images as story-starters. "Today I saw myself in a weird mirror and I looked..."

Any experience inconsistent with one's self-concept may be perceived as a threat. The more of these experiences there are, the more rigidly self-concept is organized to maintain and protect itself. When a person is unable to get rid of perceived inconsistencies, emotional problems arise.

I moved during my next-to-last-year of high school. It was hard for me, as I was shy and bookish, not the kind of kid who readily makes friends, although I wanted friends. I'll never forget hearing later from a classmate, who had gone out of her way to become my friend, that the other kids had thought me stuck up. That was one of the worst things you could be called in high school, so it really hurt. Plus, it was so wrong. I wasn't in the least bit snobbish; I was just painfully shy. It was a surprise to her, too. Once she got to know me, she knew just what I meant. I was lucky she was one kid willing to overlook the label others had put on me. That doesn't happen often, even now that I'm an adult.

—Tina P.

Faulty thinking patterns, such as dividing everything in terms of opposites or extremes, can lead to creating negative interpretations of ourselves. Our self-concept is organized. Most researchers agree self-concept has a generally stable quality. Each of us maintains countless ideas about our existence. Each idea goes down the road with all the others. It is this generally stable and organized quality of self-concept that gives consistency to the personality. It's how we know who we are. Part of how we know who we are is feedback from those around us. As John Muir said, "Everything is hitched to everything else."

TRY THIS

Talk about how self-concepts are influenced by the way others react to us. Ask students to give their reactions to the following situations:

A. You take a seat in the cafeteria but are told the seat is saved for someone else.

B. Teams are chosen for baseball and you are named captain.

C. Teams are chosen for a contest and the team captains argue about who has to take you.

(continued)

D. You are chosen "Student of the Week."

Have students in each situation describe how they would feel about others and about themselves. Particularly in A and C, point out one unpleasant reaction from someone else does not mean you have to think poorly of yourself. You can think of things you like about yourself.

Extension: Have students come up with additional scenarios.

Self-concept requires consistency and stability, and tends to resist change. If our self-concept changed too easily, we'd lack a consistent and dependable personality. Without that, we'd have a hard time relating to the world in any real sense. The more central a particular belief is to one's self-concept, the more resistant one is to changing that belief. This helps explain, in part, why battered women remain with their abusers. At heart, they have developed a self-concept that copes with their circumstances. Often this concept itself stems from low self-esteem.

We're always going to be more than the sum of our parts, but each of us copes with life in a unique way. As a species, we're remarkably resilient, adaptable, and able to hold on stubbornly to our past. If we fail in one aspect of our lives we value highly, we can look at ourselves as total losers. That spills over into other areas of our lives and everything starts to look bleak. On the other hand, when we succeed in an important area, the spillover effect brightens everything else.

To be nobody but yourself in a world
which is doing its best night and day to make
you like everybody else means to fight the hardest battle
any human being can fight and never stop fighting.

—e. e. cummings

Self-concept is dynamic. It can and does change by what we think about ourselves, how we perceive our place in the world, and what we do to alter those perceptions. To understand the active nature of self-concept, it helps to imagine it as a gyrocompass—a continuously active system that dependably points to the "true north" of a person's perceived existence. This guidance system not only shapes the ways a person views oneself, others, and the world, but it also serves to direct action and enables each person to take a consistent stance in life. Rather than viewing self-concept as the cause of behavior, it is better understood as the gyrocompass of human personality, providing consistency in personality and direction for behavior. The dynamic quality of self-concept also carries corollaries.

EYE OPENER

How much of your self-image stems from other sources, like your family? Do an inventory to figure out what labels came from where. Analyze what you want to keep and what you don't.

A friend of mine was describing his job to me, telling me how it had become set into its routine pattern, not exciting, not interesting, but not bad. "It's what I do," he said, "like you, right?" He was working that job to support himself while he was also working on establishing himself in what he really wanted to do. I was doing the same thing. My "day job" had reached a point where some days I could barely tolerate it. When he said what he did, it didn't take long for my answer. "No," I told him, "it's not what I do. It's what I'm doing to make a buck, but it's not what I do. To me, what I do means who I am, and I am not that job."

Maybe the distinction sounds petty, but not to me. If I defined myself by what I was doing then, I would just have given up. I know who I am; if I have to define myself, then I'll use the label of what I am headed for being. When I am getting paid to do what I do, then it'll be "what I do."

—Jack K.

We don't just see the world and the things in it. We see the world in relation to ourselves and our place in it. That's why it's so important to anchor ourselves with a highly developed self-concept. It's why a negative label from someone important can be so devastating. That same resilience also allows us to exclude negative input, but it can be a lengthy and painful process if the hurt is bad enough. One "you're stupid" from a parent can set a child back years, even potentially cripple a particularly sensitive individual. In the healthy personality there is constant assimilation of new ideas and expulsion of old ideas throughout life. Individuals strive to behave in ways that are in keeping with their self-concepts, no matter how helpful or hurtful to oneself or others.

Self-esteem isn't everything; it's just there's nothing without it.
—Gloria Steinem

TRY THIS

Have students draw pictures of themselves. Put names under each drawing and display them around the room for the entire week. Have the children write positive comments on each picture and talk about the uniqueness of each one.

Labels, themselves, are just words. It's our perception of those words that decide their effect. In some, they can identify a behavior or pattern of behaviors that, once recognized, can be changed. "I'm overweight," can start a campaign for healthier eating and exercise. "You're fat," could do the same but it's a hurtful label rather than a helpful one. It could even trigger the vicious cycle of eating because you're unhappy and being unhappy causes you to eat. "I'm concerned about your health," suggests a change may be in order. "You're a whale," gets you nowhere. A label can assist us in introspection, in identifying who and what we are. That can be positive. Perhaps there's something about you that you haven't recognized as a strength. Someone says to you, "You're a real workhorse. I can always depend on you to get something done." To you, getting things done is just what you do. To be called a workhorse might have offended you, but the label was put into context of someone who knows they can count on you. Suddenly, it's not so bad.

On the other hand, the stop-short nature of labels—the tendency to cut off more than they include—can also be limiting.

A routine visit to my doctor was suddenly less routine. I didn't realize it until this day, but my doctor's patter was his way of sounding me out on what else was going on in my life that might have an effect on my health. Otherwise, I was never very forthcoming. I had been trained since childhood you didn't "tell tales out of school." If things were not good at home, I'd been taught, that information stayed at home. You didn't go blabbing it everywhere. You sure didn't tell anybody like a doctor about it.

My now-ex and I had been going through some really bad stuff. He'd slapped me around a few times, like that. It sounds stupid, but I didn't even know it until later I was embarrassed about this. I was embarrassed it had happened, I was paralyzed about doing something about it. Anyway, it was my doctor who introduced me to the concept of co-dependent. I felt like a bright light had been let into my life. Suddenly, I knew why and who I was. I went right out and bought the book he recommended on the subject. It was a huge bestseller, but I had missed it. I missed all that stuff. Dismissed it out of hand as being bunk. The way I was brought up, self-awareness equaled self-indulgence.

I swung way out to the far end of that pendulum. Co-dependent central, that was me. I read the book and read it again. I adopted it like a badge. That's where I went wrong. I stopped there. "Co-dependent" took over taking charge and changing things. Other people are probably smarter than I was about it. For me it became the solution. It became me. The co-dependent label was my crutch. It excused my inaction, let me off the hook and gave me a new badge to wear. Victim had served me long enough. Eventually, I returned to the center point swing of the pendulum and figured out just identifying behaviors isn't enough. Trading one label for another doesn't accomplish anything. It might allow you to not be so hard on yourself that you don't change if you need to change.

—Ada R.

Famous people who defied their labels:

- Ray Charles was told, "you can't play the piano and God knows you can't sing."
- Fred Astaire was told he could only "dance a little."
- Beethoven was "hopeless as a composer."
- Disney "(had) no ideas."
- Caruso "(couldn't) sing."

TRY THIS

Pretend there are no other reasons *not* to do something you've always wanted to try. Shut out all the voices from your past that tell you "you can't do it...your (fill in the sibling) is the one in our family who does that...you have no talent for this...you're good at that..."

Clichés get to be clichés because there's enough truth in them to sustain the retelling. One rotten apple really can spoil the barrel. Ask any substitute teacher in the country. They can walk into any class, anywhere and in ten minutes they'll know the names of the trouble-makers. Students who are challenges are likely the ones who need lots of extra attention and support. They may have been identified—or labeled—early. Often the label sticks like glue. We'll talk more about labels in a school setting in the next chapter. There's no doubt about it: negative events can cause people to self-label. They can send us looking for acceptance in unhealthy places seeking refuge.

A woman from a solidly middle-class background suffered for years from undiagnosed mental illness. In her family, *mentally ill* meant *crazy*. Even though she suffered symptoms of severe depression early on, she was not treated. Later, as a young adult, her problems manifested themselves in an unhealthy relationship. As her condition deteriorated, she began to hallucinate. Her husband had her committed. When she was released, she came home to an empty apartment and no husband. She had no job, no family support she could claim at the time, and nowhere to go. She was homeless.

It wasn't something I would have believed. This just didn't happen to people like me. I was educated, even had my master's degree. I was on the streets. I found something there, though, as bad as it was at times, I had never felt before. I found acceptance—and love. The people on the streets took me in as part of their family. I had someplace I belonged, at last. They didn't ask questions or blame me. They just accepted me.

—Mary H.

Mary did eventually get off the streets, but her experience in finding acceptance was not unique. Teens who migrate to gangs or other alternative lifestyles such as the "Goth" movement often attribute this choice to looking for the same thing.

I got into the Gothic thing because my life at home was so awful. All my mom cared about was having somebody to clean the house and take care of my younger sister. I was wearing all this weird black makeup and all the weird clothes and stuff and she didn't do a thing. I felt like those people were my friends when I first got into it, and I have a hard time making friends, so for me, then, it was something I had always wanted. I could go down the halls at school and people would get out of my way. That was pretty cool for somebody like me, who could never get any attention before.

What got me out were the drugs. I met a girl who was a few years older than me who got really messed up with drugs—heroin and stuff like that. She got herself straightened out, but she was still a real mess. She asked me if I wanted to go to college and I said yes, because it's always been my dream to go to college. She told me, "Then you better get out of this while you can. You stay here, you aren't going to college." I believed her, and I got out. It was enough for me.

—Crystal B.

Self-fulfilling prophecy has been with us at least since the time of the ancient Greeks. As the story goes, the sculptor Pygmalion, a prince of Cyprus, sought to create an ivory statue of the ideal woman. He named his sculpture Galatea. She was so beautiful that Pygmalion fell passionately in love with his own creation. He prayed to the goddess Venus to bring Galatea to life. Venus granted his prayer and the couple lived happily ever after. The play *Pygmalion* by Bernard Shaw, and the musical made from the play, *My Fair Lady*, have given rise to what some sociologists call the Pygmalion effect. Eliza Doolittle tells Pickering she will always be a flower girl to Professor Higgins because he will always treat her as such. She correctly noted his perceptions of her favor his expectations.

A study was conducted at the University of South Florida to investigate self-fulfilling prophecy and its effect on performance. This time the study was not on academic classroom performance, but with a sports class. A group of beginning tennis players was divided into three groups. The first group was told they could control their abilities and effort and could change their performance. The second was told their failures were because of a lack of innate ability. The third group was told nothing at all. At the conclusion of the study, the first group scored consistently higher in all measured categories. You could say they were given a positive label and had direct bearing on the outcome.

TRY THIS

I Cheer for Myself! Start each day by leading a cheer for one student. Example: Justin, "Give me a J ... give me a U..." spelling child's name. "What do you have?" Class responds by shouting child's name. Cheer for a different child each day.

A "no" uttered from deepest conviction is better and greater than a "yes" merely uttered to please, or what is worse, to avoid trouble.

—Mahatma Gandhi

Self-fulfilling prophecies can have a great deal of power over our behavior. Once an expectation is set, even if it's not accurate, we tend to act in ways that help us bring a prophecy to fruition.

I've always had a weight problem. Like a lot of people, I eat when things are bothering me. When I tried to lose weight, I always told myself that because I ate when I was upset, I was also telling myself this was something I could not change. Bingo. I couldn't. So naturally I didn't lose weight.

Eventually I joined one of those weight control groups. A combination of that and just hitting the right point in my life turned me around. I figured out I had been fooling myself for a long time. I could indeed stop eating just because I was upset. It sounds foolish, but that had not occurred to me. It had really never occurred to me this behavior was up for grabs. It was exciting. I could control other things too. Wow! I just wonder why nobody ever clued me in to this before. Does everybody have to figure this out the hard way? I sure hope not.

—Katherine J.

EYE OPENER

A scrawny tenth- grader, called "ugly" by his schoolmates, was invited to join the track team. Though shy, self-conscious and lacking confidence, he accepted the invitation and began throwing the javelin. He practiced every night. He even set a national high school record. He took an unexpected turn into acting when a torn shoulder muscle ended his javelin throwing career. Eventually, that ugly young man starred in *Bonanza* and *Little House on the Prairie*. Who was he? Michael Landon.

As a boy, he was beaten frequently by his father and told he had no brains. He drifted from school to school. Along the way he was advised to pursue a career repairing elevators. However, a night at the boxing arena changed his life forever. He saw Chuck Wepner go the distance with Muhammad Ali, despite the fearful beating Ali was dishing out. Wepner inspired this admirer, Sylvester Stallone, to write the script for *Rocky*, the movie that launched his career in film.

In short, don't believe everything you hear.

TRY THIS

Pick a label that could help you take a new direction in your life. Maybe you've always wanted to paint. Start each morning saying "I am a painter." Then paint, if only for ten minutes. Can you create another Last Supper in this fashion? No, but you can take a serious, committed step to creating the reality of the label you want.

Research on the role of gender in self-esteem has revealed some interesting information. Even the best teachers have been observed treating boys and girls differently in the classroom. Boys who answered questions correctly, for instance, were usually presented with follow-up questions that would further probe the depth of knowledge. Girls usually were not.

So often we measure our own self-worth by comparing ourselves to others. This type of valuation usually shows us on the wrong side of the comparison. If, by chance, we do come out favorably that success is justified with an excuse like "Yes, I am better at this than so-and-so, but I had the advantage of taking this class." You lose again. There is nothing wrong with valuing yourself just for you. We all say "I *should* do this" or "I *should* do that." Instead, replace *should* with words like *want*, *choose* or *prefer*. It's a simple change. It sounds like a small one, but it's one that will raise your self-esteem. These are action words. Action instead of passive reaction is a first-rate self-esteem raiser.

---

cried the third crumb, I am should
and this is my little sister could
with our big brother who is would
don't punish us for we were good;

—e.e. cummings

Whether consciously or not, we tip people off as to what our expectations are. We exhibit thousands of cues, some as subtle as tilting our heads, and people pick up on those cues. This behavior can create a self-fulfilling loop. We give signals, people pick up on them, and we get the feedback we're asking for on whatever level and start all over again.

TRY THIS

For adults: Take some time to stop periodically throughout the day to be aware of what signals you might be giving. Are they ones you'd choose if you were more aware? If not, what would you change?

For adults and older learners: Are you trying to project confidence? Check your posture. People who slump don't project confidence. Do you look people in the eyes? In Western culture, confident people look each other in the eyes (without staring, but look at people eye-to-eye). Be sensitive to the customs of other cultures, where this behavior is considered rude or otherwise inappropriate.

A man's reach should exceed his grasp, or what's a Heaven for?
—Robert Louis Stevenson

EYE OPENER

For older students and adults: Explore the quote by Stevenson. It should provide fodder for a wide-ranging discussion.

The label *impossible* has been thrown at too many who try to stretch. It's a negative, defeating view. It's true if you decide you want to pilot an F18 at age sixty, you may have chosen a stretch that's just unrealistic. If you decide you want to go back to college at forty-five years old, you'll find naysayers, but it can be accomplished. If you're from a poor family and want to attend an Ivy League school, you've got challenges ahead, but you can accomplish this, too.

Stretch your foot to the length of your blanket.

—Persian proverb

TRY THIS

Have students create new proverbs similar to the Persian one above. Discuss what proverbs are and how they inspire us. The proverbs they write will be ones that will urge them, and their peers, to strive to be the best they can be. Write the new proverbs on special paper and decorate the room with them.

Encourage students to stretch as far as they can.

A teacher who, however well-intentioned, tries to put limits on a student can do more damage than they are trying to prevent. A parent who says, "You can't do that," does the same. It may be a balancing act to try to assess whether or not someone has a realistic chance of success, but isn't the journey as important as the destination?

I was very unsure I could succeed. I had picked something very risky to try, after all, and I had small children to support. It hit me one day, I would never have another time to try. I could wait until they were grown and gone, sure. My family and friends were all for that road, but it wasn't for me. Sometimes, when I was up late at night, I thought about giving in to common sense. I hate common sense! If I had listened to it, I would not be on the verge of breaking into selling a motion picture script. I had to shut off a lifetime of listening to people telling me the right thing to do, of always being responsible. I had worn "responsible" like a badge my whole life. All it had seemed to get me was doing what everybody else expected of me. I was hitting forty with no clue as to what I wanted.

And I thought, too, I would be a really sad role model for my kids to give up on something just because it was a huge challenge, and something few succeeded in accomplishing. I still don't know if it was just pure stubbornness that moved me on, or a ferocious desire to show everybody they were wrong, or a terrific motivation for my kids to be proud of me. I do remember thinking I knew, I just knew if I didn't try I would regret it the rest of my life. I remember thinking it was high time for me to believe in me. I had what I thought was a really good idea. I wanted somebody else to validate that idea; that had always been important to me. I didn't get that for a while, but it didn't stop me. That's what I am the most happy about accomplishing.

That's what helps me every time my kids say "I can't do this." It gave me great ammunition.

—Paula C.

TRY THIS

When was the last time you did a *personality stretch?* When did you last try something that put you outside your comfort zone? If you've made a mistake recently, maybe it means you're finding your way as you learn some new things. Make a goal to learn one new thing a week, a day, whatever you can manage in order to stretch, learn, and grow. Guaranteed to dim the me-versus-the-world blues!

Challenge students to stretch. Make it a class goal as well as an individual goal. Have students write a "stretch" at the beginning of the school year. They can keep it secret if they want to, or they can ask for help. Have them write other stretches, smaller ones, as you go along.

My teacher told me he didn't think I would be able to make up all the work I had missed. At first I was sad because I already had a hard time because I have a learning disability. Then my friend said she would help me study. Her mom told me I could do it, and she said she would help too. I kinda got mad at my teacher, but I didn't say that. I just studied real hard and guess what? I made it! I made up all my work, got caught up and even got a "B" for that semester. That was the best I ever did in that class. Guess I showed him!

—Jesse R.

Go confidently in the direction of your dreams. Live the life you have imagined.

—Henry David Thoreau

TRY THIS

Many of us were admonished growing up, not to toot our own horns. Wasn't it just confidence and positive self-esteem? Let your student toot away! Have them name some accomplishment of which they're proud. If somebody is stuck, work with him or her until you ferret out something. Some may need help figuring out they *have* accomplished something. Little ones can be proud of riding a bike or learning to tie shoelaces. Older students can be proud of themselves for helping to look after siblings, by taking responsibility for their homework or other tasks. We all need to know there aren't necessarily going to be trophies or medals for what we accomplish. For younger learners, make horn- or trumpet-shaped templates on which they can write their accomplishment.

Extension: Institute an "Every Day Hero Award." Make certificates for things students might not think are a big deal, like those described above. Another extension is to find recordings of various types of music for several types of horns to play while the students are working. If your schedule allows, you might be able to work in a music lesson or two as well.

Part of what we learn at school is getting along with other people. One good way to do that, of course, is to talk to them and find out more about them. This exercise will enable students to get to know their classmates a bit better.

TRY THIS

Have students work with partners and each finish the following sentences:
1. An important thing to know about me is _____ .
2. I felt proud when I _____ .
3. Other people like me because I am _____ .
4. The thing I do best is _____ .
5. I look _____ .
6. If a new friend came to visit, the first thing I'd show him or her is my ____ .
7. I like myself because _____ .
8. I do not feel important when _____ .

Students should exchange their papers to read their partner's answers. Conclude by asking, "What is the most important thing you learned about your partner?" If time permits, have the partners share this information with the class. Be sensitive to any child who is adamant about not sharing information with the class.

Me, Myself, and I

All the time I was growing up, my mother told me I didn't have any common sense. This usually happened when I did something in my own way instead of the way she wanted me to do it, especially if she hadn't said how she wanted it done. Or it might happen if I didn't do something she wanted. Or if I just thought for myself. This was lose-lose for me. I lost all the way round. It took me years to figure out common sense was only common if both parties in a conversation knew what the other was talking about. Eventually I figured out I had just as much common sense as anyone else. What was really funny was, as soon as I was pregnant with my first child, I suddenly had lots of common sense. Go figure.

—Carol C.

That kind of life is most happy which affords us most opportunities of gaining our own self-esteem.

—Samuel Johnson

Public opinion is a weak tyrant compared with our own private opinion. What a man thinks of himself, that is which determines, or rather indicates, his fate.

—Henry David Thoreau

Self-esteem, particularly in teenagers, is often bound up in body image. Dieting, weight preoccupation, and eating disorders during adolescence are associated with poor body image, higher incidence of substance use and increased social isolation. It's estimated by psychologists that somewhere between 60 and 80 percent of adolescent and high school girls want to lose weight.

TRY THIS

For older students: Discuss self-esteem and its relationship to personal appearance. Have students fill out this survey.

1. I am _____ .
2. I want to change _____ .
3. I feel _____ about my appearance.
4. I need to lose _____ pounds. (zero is an acceptable answer)
5. I care what my friends think of how I look. _____Yes _____ No

—(continued)—

6. I would change something about my appearance if my friends thought
I should: _____ Yes _____ No

Tally the results of the poll and share them with the class. Discuss the outcome. Have students create additional questions to be asked.

Know thyself.
—Inscribed on the temple of Apollo at Delphi

Self-esteem is a concept the current generation of schoolchildren knows well. In young children, self-esteem refers to the extent to which they expect to be accepted and valued by adults and peers who are important to them. There is no doubt, if they have not heard this term before starting school, they will certainly do so after they start. What is true self-esteem and how do we teach children they can build it? All children, all of our students, should come to class knowing they will be respected and valued for themselves and teachers care about them and their progress. Genuine self-esteem, however, will come from certain knowledge we help children acquire. If they feel confident they have the skills to deal with life, the ability to test themselves and the confidence to face challenges, they will have genuine self-esteem. If they use the skills to accomplish things, they will have genuine self-esteem and the ability to withstand the ebb and flow of their lives.

A lot of my friends are panicking. They don't have a clue. They're seniors and they haven't even started looking for colleges or anything. They might not even be able to go for a year or two after high school. I'm a junior, and I'm starting now. My dad has been telling me and telling me I've got to think farther than the end of my nose. It sounds corny, but I finally got the message. I don't want to be caught short when it's time to graduate. I never thought of myself as somebody who could do that kind of planning. It didn't seem like me. It's beginning to now. It's given me another way to think about myself. I like it.
—High school girl

Never bend your head. Hold it high. Look the world straight in the eye.
—Helen Keller

Planning for the future takes foresight, time, and effort. It's not a skill or a concept all young people have, no matter how hard we try to get the message across. It's a skill guaranteed to pay off dividends in self-esteem, even if the complete payoff is somewhere down the road. Self-esteem is most likely to be fostered when children are esteemed by the adults who are important to them. To esteem children means to treat them respectfully, ask their views and opinions, take them seriously, and give them meaningful and realistic feedback.

TO THINK ABOUT

When was the last time you *really* listened to a child in the same way you would like others to listen to you?

Healthy self-esteem is developed and maintained by helping children cope with defeat, rather than emphasizing constant success and triumph. During times of disappointment or crisis, children need to know their weakened self-esteem can be strengthened by letting them know your love and support remain unchanged.

TRY THIS

For younger learners: The next time you've had a bad day at work, or the class is not going well on a particular day, tell the child how you feel—that you're having a bad day. Teachers, you may need to wait until you and your class have had a chance to get to know each other. You may be surprised at the level of understanding that will come back to you.

When the crisis has passed, help the child reflect on what went wrong. The next time a crisis occurs, he or she can use the knowledge gained from overcoming past difficulties to help cope with a new crisis. A child's sense of self-worth and self-confidence is not likely to deepen when adults deny life has its ups and downs. This includes, for children, times when they feel picked on at school, or when name-calling may be something they're dealing with on a daily basis.

Chapter Four

School Days

Interpreting physics problems and reading music are very much alike in that they are both learned skills—and you can learn anything you want to learn. What you learn depends ultimately on you.

— Ronald Brown, Physics Department
Cal Poly, San Luis Obispo

Chicken and the Lake

All the animals of both the forest and farm knew very well that Owl was wise, and the one to ask if there were great questions to be answered. It was just as well known that Chicken was foolish and scatter-brained and the one to be avoided when great questions needed to be answered. It happened that one day Chicken left the farmyard and undertook a journey into the forest where, she had heard, there was a small, but beautiful lake full of cool clear water.

Chicken walked and walked. At last, she came to the top of a long hill. From here, she looked down into a lush valley. Still she saw no lake.

"They are right when they say I am foolish," she cried. "There is no lake!"

Just as she said these words, a tiny voice behind her said, "Touch the rock at your side three times and you will find what you seek."

Chicken did as the voice bid her and, suddenly, in the valley was the cool clear lake she sought. She leapt for joy, and was about to run to enjoy the water, when she turned to see who had helped her.

74

It was a mouse. Chicken thanked her heartily.

"Just remind your friends, if they should come," said the mouse, after Chicken had thanked her. "If they don't touch the magic rock, they will not find the lake." With that, she scampered off into the woods.

When she returned home, Chicken told all her friends about the lake. They were all eager to see it for themselves. Owl and Cat both decided they would make the journey.

As the road wore one both became weary, even Owl, who flew high above Cat.

"I'm going on ahead," declared Owl. "Chicken is foolish. Magic rocks indeed!" So, on he flew, with no lake in sight, no matter how high and far he flew. Cat grew tired, but he kept on. At last, he came to the top of the high hill where he, too, saw the rock. He did as Chicken had told him and he, too, was rewarded as the lake revealed itself. He ran down to enjoy a drink from the cool water.

Meanwhile, Owl had returned home, angry at not finding the lake and determined to tease Chicken about once again being so foolish.

"Chicken," he began, "you sent us on a wasted journey. There was no lake."

The other animals started to laugh at foolish Chicken.

"Oh, but there was!" purred Cat. "Did you touch the rock like Chicken said? I did. I had a lovely drink. I even dangled my paws in the water, and you know how cats hate to get wet."

"Well, er, uh, no. I didn't," admitted Owl.

"Then you should have paid attention," said Cat.

We can learn from any teacher, if only we listen.

If our families introduce us to labeling, our schools are next in line to take up the job. What we learn at home will be reinforced at school, usually by classmates echoing what they've learned, eager to pass along the hurt and pain of being called names. Our classmates may well have new names in store for us. Given recent tragic events committed by students who claim an unbearable level of torment from this type of labeling, perhaps it's time to consider new tactics to change the way our students deal with each other.

EYE OPENER

What was the popular name to call people when you were in elementary school, middle school, and high school? Are those names popular today? What is the policy regarding name-calling at the school your children attend or where you teach?

I'm really embarrassed about it now that I think about it but, when I was in eighth grade, the big thing to call each other, (especially somebody you didn't like), was retard. The way we pronounced it sounded more like retart. We knew retard was an abbreviation of retarded. After a while, our word came to be just a generalized insult. It didn't have a thing to do with being retarded.

—Jim P.

A co-worker's daughter has Down's syndrome. She refers to her daughter as being retarded, because she is. She's not sensitive about that because she's so practical about just making sure her daughter works up to whatever potential she has. She's very clear about what her girl can and cannot do. Me, on the other hand, practically an adopted auntie, I am very sensitive about anybody calling her names or anything.

I don't hear that label much any more. Maybe once in a while, but not like when I was a kid. The teachers at my children's schools are very sensitive about names like that, and they put a stop to it. They work with the kids a lot with regards to that kind of thing. Sometimes I think they go overboard. I mean, it almost gets to the point it seems ridiculous, but then I think: no. This kind of thing has to stop somewhere. Some time. It may take a whole lot more generations working on it, but it's the only way we can stop hurting each other with names and labels.

—Karen R.

Give everyone a chance. Just keep an open mind. You just never know what somebody will be like unless you give them a chance.
—Eight grader, promotion address

I pay the schoolmaster, but it's the schoolboys that educate my son.
—Ralph Waldo Emerson

76

In some ways, things have not changed since Emerson's time. The kinds of lessons he referred to with regard to his son are still being taught. A week after the shooting at Santana High School in California, legislation was passed by the Washington State Senate requiring each of the state's 296 school districts to adopt strict policies against harassment, intimidation, and bullying. The measure also required districts to train staff members to spot and deal with bullying. The dissenting votes came from Republicans, who felt there was no way to legislate against this kind of behavior. They pointed out these types of policies and procedures were already in place at Santana, however, they had not prevented the shootings.

Walk onto any elementary school playground or middle school or high school hallways during passing period and you'll hear lots of name-calling. Some of it might make you blush. Some of it's posturing. Some of it's just silly. Lots of it has just one aim—to taunt, tease, and make somebody's life miserable. Andy Williams was not the first adolescent to claim he snapped under an incessant barrage of teasing. Ironically, a little over a year after Andy's shooting spree, he had sprouted into a tall, broad shouldered young man who looked like a football player. The physical attributes that seemed to have triggered the teasing had vanished with a little time.

Bullying, teasing, name-calling, labeling—whatever guise the behavior takes—has been around since there were people. Early man probably called each other "buffalo breath." Why does it happen? Usually, the person throwing the names around is unhappy. They call you a name, and bingo, they feel a bit more powerful because they dumped on you and had a powerful effect on you. I put my unhappiness on you. If you react, you take it on. On the other hand, if you don't react the way I want, I get more unhappy. Not only have I failed to dump my state of mind on you, but I've failed at making you unhappy.

TRY THIS

Superhero Awards: The theme of this concept is "I Have the Power to Help." Have the kids reward each other by giving out Superhero Power Buttons every time they have positive comments for classmates.

Insults and taunting are as common as not having adults who take them seriously. We must all keep our ears open. If a student complains of being teased to the extent life is becoming miserable, take it seriously. Alert other teachers to the problem. Try to monitor the student's interactions with others. Some students are more sensitive than others. Perhaps he or she needs help with coping skills. Perhaps the teasers need help developing sensitivity toward others. Never ignore a child who's complaining of being teased. They might just need a receptive ear.

Insults take many forms. They all hurt. Racial, ethnic, and sexual slurs are particularly abusive because they reflect a history of oppression, and therefore there is more power to inflict damage with such slurs. Children don't need to be reminded they are members of a denigrated class.

EYE OPENER

Do you think it's possible to eliminate racial and ethnic stereotyping in this generation? Or at all?

TRY THIS

Ask students the same question. Ask them how they think the world would change if they could snap their fingers and magically make racism and labeling disappear.

Teachers open the door, but you must enter by yourself.
—Chinese Proverb

Sometimes slurs are not even recognized as being hurtful and may be considered socially acceptable. Many young people use terms such as nigger, epic, faggot, lezzie, or queer because they know the effectiveness of their hurtful nature. The use of slurs attack another's self-esteem and teach young people that hatred of one group is condoned by our society. For adolescents in the surge of hormones, labels related to emerging sexuality are among the most common.

TRY THIS

Have students brainstorm names they have been called or heard others being called. List all the names on the board. Reluctant students may need encouraging to say these names aloud. Reassure them frank and open discussion is not the same thing as actually using the names.

—(continued)—

> *For older learners:* Discuss categories of racial, ethnic, sexual or religious bias. Place the names you've come up with accordingly.
>
> *For younger learners:* Talk about why names hurt. Lead students to an awareness that all name-calling involves prejudice and is equally bad. Be clear none of the listed names is acceptable in your classroom. Make it clear you will not tolerate any form of name-calling. Explain why and discuss consequences for failure to adhere to this rule.

Although name-calling often attacks students at a distinctly personal level (with regard to appearance, ethnicity, religion, and sexual orientation) labels also arise from levels of achievement. Group instruction, though it has definite advantages in the classroom, can also give rise to labeling. Students will be aware of ability grouping. It's important children are made to understand everyone has different abilities and strengths. It's part of the teacher's job to ensure each child contributes to the classroom in his or her own unique fashion.

It is our choices, Harry, that show what we truly are, far more than our abilities.

—Professor Dumbledore, character from J. K. Rowling's, *Harry Potter and the Chamber of Secrets*

TRY THIS

What are your school's expectations with regard to labeling? Are there consequences in place for those who don't respect the rules? Is there a classroom policy with regard to labeling?

For teachers: Involve your students in creating a code of conduct. Create banners, stickers, posters, and other artwork to express a positive way to deal with each other. Involve other aspects of your curriculum whenever possible.

Why discuss teacher expectations in a book on labeling? Teacher expectations can *become* labels. The issue is raised here only to keep the awareness level high regarding the possibility.

In one review of a teacher expectation study, an estimated five to ten percent variation in student performance can be traced to different treatment based on their teachers' expectations of them. Five to ten percent is hardly the epidemic of mistreatment and negative outcomes perceived by some educators and members of the general public. However, when compounded through years of schooling, it is significant enough to warrant concern. Researchers have also found younger children are more susceptible to the effects of expectancy communications than older students and communicating low expectations seems to have more power on lowering student performance than communicating high expectations has on raising performance.

Much literature on teacher expectations calls attention to the fact students do, in fact, have different ability levels and require different instructional approaches, materials, and rates. None of the research suggests teachers should hold the same expectations for all students, nor that they should deliver identical instruction to them all. Rather, they focus on the problems created when differential treatment either creates or sustains differences in student performance that would probably not exist if students were treated more equitably.

Although it would be misleading and inaccurate to say teacher expectations determine a student's success, research clearly establishes teacher expectations do play a significant role in determining how well and how much students learn. The second type of expectation involves a teacher's prediction about how much academic progress a student will make over a specified period of time. It appears *expected* improvement is only weakly correlated with a teacher's present assessment of the student.

I have the same teacher for social studies my sister had. The teacher called me "Elizabeth's brother." My sister did really well in that class. I'm good in that subject too, but my sister and I are not the same. My mom told me the teacher is really good, and that she was just teasing me, and she's probably right, but I sure hope she starts calling me by my name.

—Alex Y., Eighth grader

Another study found students labeled *slow* may receive fewer opportunities to learn new material than students labeled *bright*, and slow students typically are taught less difficult material. The effect of such behavior is cumulative and, over time, teachers' predictions of student achievement may become true. The third type of expectation is the degree to which a teacher over or underestimates a student's present level of performance. This type of expectation results from a teacher's estimate of student ability based upon some formal assessment of the student's performance. It is most often driven by the use of a test that is perceived to provide an accurate measure of student ability.

These findings are significant, particularly in light of evidence suggesting a student often internalizes teachers' expectations over time. When this internalization occurs, the student's self-concept and motivation to achieve may decline. Evidence clearly shows low teacher expectations for students can negatively affect student performance. Meanwhile, evidence of high expectations for students having an impact has been just as clearly documented.

When I was doing my student teaching, one of my professors was fond of saying, in his opinion, kindergarten teachers should get paid twice as much as college professors-himself included. In fact he felt the pay scale should start at the highest point there and go down as the grade level increased. He believed because the kindergarten teacher got a hold of kids at the start of their educational careers, their influence was the most potent and most likely to set the stage for the rest of school.

—Linda A.

If the condition of man is to be progressively ameliorated, as we fondly hope and believe, education is to be the chief instrument in effecting it...I look to the diffusion of light and education as the resource most to be relied on for ameliorating the condition, promoting the virtue, and advancing the happiness of man.

—Thomas Jefferson

I had a kid in my class once who was very tall for his age, and he was also extremely articulate. Sometimes without realizing it, you can't help it—you start expecting a lot more from a kid like that, because he looks older, and at times he sounds older. Then you have to take a step back and remind yourself just how old he is, and what that means in terms of his classmates. He has the same basic social skills they do. He's not any more mature because he looks like he could be. It's easy to make snap judgments. You have to be able to snap back just as fast, though. It's fun, at the end of the school year, to look back and see what has happened over the course of my time with the kids. I think the most fun comes when you think back to that first "take" on a student. Did he or she surprise you? The surprises have often been, for me, the most rewarding part of teaching.

—Judy J.

When I taught fourth grade, I had a kid in my class, Joey, who was the classic "class clown." I'd heard all about him, of course, before I met him. He had a reputation. I may be as bad as he was, but I thought he was kind of funny. That aside, I knew he needed to learn how to get along in school so his life wouldn't be miserable. He just wasn't really very interested in school at the time, though he could be a bright student when something caught his interest.

One day I had an inspiration. We were writing "tall tales"— Paul Bunyan stuff. The kids were making up their own. Joey's was terrific, not surprising. Who else would be as good at making up tall stories?! Anyway, the librarian learned about what we were doing and asked if I would send a couple of kids over with some of the kids' work to put on display. We had written the stories on adding machine tape, so they were tall physically, too.

I decided to send Joey on this (for fourth-graders) prestigious assignment. The librarian had her concerns, and a few of the other teachers thought I was nuts, I know. I hedged my bets and sent along as his helper Frank, the most stolid, quiet boy in the class, a generally serious boy who would be the least likely candidate to indulge in the horseplay I knew Joey would at the first opportunity. I figured Frank would slow him down.

It turned out Joey didn't need his shadow after all. He was so conscious of the importance of getting this plum job, and keeping it, he was the model student. The librarian could hardly tell it was the same kid. I asked her how he had done and she told me he had gone right to work putting up the stories, making sure the display looked as good as it could, and helping Frank in his part of the job, too. Thank goodness she too realized the impact this assignment had on Joey.

She just thanked him for his good work and didn't comment on how she had expected him to cut up.

Joey was different from then on. He didn't give up being the class clown, but he started being better able to manage himself, and occasionally reign in an inappropriate comment, or keep his mouth shut during visits from the principal, or others, which would have raised some eyebrows, at least for the most part. He offered to help more in the class, too, which was new for him. He even wanted to go out for Safety Patrol, but I knew the other teachers would veto that idea. Those jobs go to the kids who never get into the slightest scrape with authority. The funny thing was Joey would have been the best kid on the squad. He wanted it so much, he would have toed the line. He would have been conscientious to a fault.

We had a new understanding between us after the library thing. He was grateful I'd given him a position of trust. He couldn't say it in words, but he did in deed, and that spoke more to me than anything he could have said. I'll never forget the look of pride in his eyes when I praised him. Most teachers will tell you they learn as much from their students as they ever teach them. Joey was no exception. He taught me about looking past the labels, even if sometimes you're going in blind. You just never know what you'll find. I found a new label for Joey: responsible. He liked that one.

—Nina P.

Education is the movement from darkness to light.

—Allan Bloom

TO THINK ABOUT

For teachers: Do you have any "Joey" students? Are there activities or responsibilities he or she could try to bolster a sense of responsibility?

For parents: Can you create opportunities for your own children to shine you might not have considered before?

For all adults: Can you think of a time when someone took a chance on you? If you can, then you know the boost it affords when another places faith in you. See if you can create a self-fulfilling prophecy of success in someone else.

A great way to provide some productive labeling is to take Dr. Howard Gardner's *Theory of Multiple Intelligences* into the classroom— and home, too! It provides information to help children learn more effectively. Dr. Gardner outlined eight different intelligences to account for human potential. See if you can recognize your child's style from the following descriptions. Adapt forays into learning, accommodating individual style. Share helpful information with your child's teacher. Remember, all children work well with hands-on activities and manipulatives.

TO THINK ABOUT

For parents: Of the names assigned by Gardner's conception of intelligence listed below, which describes your child's primary mode of learning?

For teachers: Do you know the primary learning mode for each child in your class? Do you incorporate this into your lesson planning? What are your strategies for encouraging each type of learner?

- Linguistic intelligence—word smart
- Logical-mathematical intelligence—number/reasoning smart
- Spatial intelligence—picture smart
- Bodily-kinesthetic intelligence—body smart
- Musical intelligence—music smart
- Interpersonal intelligence—people smart
- Intra-personal intelligence—self smart
- Naturalist intelligence—nature smart

The first day of school I received "homework" from my son's P.E. coach. I admit to being a bit irked—it had already been a long day and he wanted me to write a letter about my son, explaining strengths and weaknesses, likes and dislikes in school—any relevant information I thought would help him to get to know my son better. As I wrote, not only did I reinforce my own notion of what a neat and interesting person my son was, I realized here was a teacher who really believed in knowing the whole child, not just what he saw on the field, and by writing this, I was helping him gain insights. My irritation vanished, replaced by gratitude.

—Hilda F.

Identifying learning styles and adapting lesson plans accordingly can help eliminate unfair labeling. By using these labels, teachers and parents will have a much easier time finding ways to praise children. They put concrete terms on qualities parents and teachers may appreciate in children but have a hard time putting into words. According to Dr. Gardner, the school system has traditionally rewarded primarily the linguistic and logical-mathematical learners. Other means of achievement have not been recognized nearly as often or as eagerly. The good news is, by recognizing and rewarding other forms of relating to the world, we have a much greater chance of realizing the potential of many more students. By doing this we afford a greater avenue for students to realize greater self-esteem. Students with higher self-esteem are more confident and less likely to be targets of labeling and name-calling.

Remember, too, children can be dominant in one style or use a combination of styles. We can aid them by targeting their strongest modes when acquiring new concepts then, by gently stretching their abilities and providing activities that incorporate other styles. This teaches them about ways in which others think and learn, a valuable skill in dealing with others, now and as adults.

TRY THIS

See how many different ways you can come up with to teach the same lesson or get across the same message. For teachers this might mean different workstations. Adults can find this useful in conversation, particularly with those they know well, and with their own children. By identifying a child's primary learning style, parents can adapt their styles to meet the needs of the situation.

Education is the ability to listen to almost anything without losing your temper or your self-confidence.
—Robert Frost

TRY THIS

For older learners: Use the Frost quote above as a conversation starter with your class. Explore how especially pertinent it is to the art of debating. Challenge the students. Do they consider themselves educated by this definition? If so, what are the biggest influences in helping to mold this thinking? If not, why not? Do they ever see this changing in their lives?

It would be nearly impossible to talk about schools without addressing testing. Why talk about testing when the overall subject is labeling? It's quite simple. Testing has a whole class of labels associated with it, and those labels are the subjects of much heated wrangling. There are few people who have not heard, or do not chant, the mantra of test scores. Schools, as well as individuals, are labeled for good and for ill. Funding can rest on the outcome of testing. Underperforming schools can lose money and students.

The public's view is clear, most Americans favor student testing for purposes of information, accountability, and incentives. It's also a great source of fodder for labeling by adults. Schools are labeled in a variety of ways—successful, unsuccessful, underachieving. Most policy makers like testing for the same reason. Much less work is required in assigning money and other resources based on test results than exploring individual differences that would explain those results. Hence, statewide assessment systems are now the norm. Most of these systems rely, to some degree, on standardized testing. What is the public fascination with testing? Maybe it's one way of dealing with what's perceived as a grand failure of the public schools. We are a nation fond of blaming. Testing is a great way to smack some blame down on somebody, whether or not it's deserved. It's also a way out of taking individual responsibility as parents.

I was checking out private schools for my daughter and was on a tour with the principal of one of the schools I was considering. She had just taken me out to the play yard. A little girl, who must only have been in the kindergarten, ran up to one of the teachers, sobbing. The teacher immediately dropped down so she was eye to eye with the child. That really impressed me. The girl was small for her age anyway, and the fact that she didn't have to look so far up was a tremendous comfort. The teacher put her arms around the child and asked what was wrong. Within a minute, the tears were gone and the smile was back. The girl scampered away, happy to rejoin her classmates. I checked out other schools, but this was where I came back to.

—Ruth H.

What is the perfect school? Have students discuss and develop their ideas of the perfect school. Every class has one (or a few) who will say there is *no* perfect school. Discuss the reality that some kind of school is a necessity. Other than that, just about anything goes. They can make models, cut out pictures from magazines, and write stories.

The stakes attached to test results are becoming more serious. Promotion and graduation often hinge on attaining a minimum score. More attention is understandably being paid to the strengths and weaknesses of standardized testing and ways of improving them. Many jurisdictions strive to make their assessments more sophisticated and sensitive. Some states supplement their standardized tests with more complex methods for gauging student, school, and district performance.

A teacher affects eternity; he can never tell where his influence stops.
—Henry Brooks Adams

The critics are relentless. Although the public and our elected officials want testing regimens to become more important, many educators hate them. In the widening use of such tests, they see a practice that distorts the curriculum, discourages higher-order thinking skills, and reduces student achievement. Teachers must devote inordinate amounts of instructional time preparing for testing. It's called *teaching to the test*. Ironically, they'll deny it if asked. They're not supposed to be doing it. They're supposed to be teaching the mandated curriculum. Unfortunately, teachers know if they don't prepare kids for standardized tests, their results may hinder the school or the district. Testing has created a perfect Catch-22.

Given the documented effects of the overuse and abuses of standardized testing, a few stalwarts maintain the routine use of such tests is ill advised. Routine uses include administration of standardized "readiness" tests or screening tests for all children entering kindergarten, and standardized achievement tests associated with state or federal preventive/remedial programs for all children beginning in second grade or earlier. These policies are based on unfounded as-sumptions that any and all children may be unable to succeed in programs that are presumably designed for typically performing chil-dren in the given age range.

When my daughter was in first grade, I offered to help her teacher when she had to administer their first test. It was nuts. In the first place, she had a bunch of kids who couldn't even master the concept of "bubbling in" the answers on the answer sheet. It got worse. The questions were so far out in left field some of the concepts wouldn't be covered until third or fourth grade. These poor children were hope-lessly confused. I wasn't far behind them, wondering what are they hoping to do with this nonsense? The teacher had to grin and bear it and do the best she could. What a complete waste of time and re-sources.

—Janet G.

Testing underwent a boom in the 1970s and 1980s and still occu-pies a central position in schools. By one estimate, the 41 million schoolchildren in America take 127 million tests annually—for some students that's as many as 12 standardized tests each year. Aside from the issue of cost-effectiveness, the cumulative effects of such ubiqui-tous testing include negative effects on students' attitudes and motivation as they proceed through school.

Several important steps can be taken to reduce the chances stan-dardized tests will dominate the curriculum and cause children to think what matters most is what is on the test. Researchers offer these recom-mendations to protect young children from inappropriate expectations, practices, and policies:

- Delay standardized testing for all children until third grade or later.
- When using standardized achievement tests for purposes of account-ability for school and district comparisons, use sampling techniques instead of testing all children.
- Schedule testing in the fall, rather than spring, so teachers will not teach to the test and scores cannot be used for teacher evaluation.

Note: The latter two phenomena have been indicted as abuse and misuse of tests for assessing young children.

TRY THIS

> On testing days, bring containers of bubbles to the classroom. After you are finished testing for the day, allow kids to blow off steam by blowing bubbles. If this is not practical for your situation, show a movie and bring popcorn or another enjoyable reward. This can be done on a small scale every day and at the end (if it's a series) have a big blowout for having worked so hard!

Teachers must work extremely hard to find where each child is, and to decide which of many possible approaches will best help that child learn. Schools are not factories; test scores are not products. No test, no matter how well designed, will ever reveal who a child is. [emphasis added]

—Steve Cohen, Lecturer, Dept. of
Education, Tufts University

There's always the odd man out who, for whatever reason, doesn't mind testing at all. This young student, in his school's Gifted and Talented Education (G.A.T.E.) program, felt at odds even among his gifted classmates. For this youngster, even the challenge of an enriched program was not enough to occupy a rapidly moving intelligence.

I love testing days. I know most kids don't, but not me. I think it's fun. I get to just have fun showing what I know. I'm not bragging or anything, because for me it's just a lot of fun. I go so fast through the tests, and they're not even hard. I wish we could have testing all the time.

—Doug Y., Sixth grader

Teacher expectations are defined as "inferences teachers make about present and future academic achievement and general classroom behavior of students" (either as a class or as individuals). General class expectations stem from a teacher's perception of changeability or rigidity of students' abilities, students' potential to benefit from instruction, appropriate difficulty of material for the class and whether the class should be taught as a group or individually. Expectations for individual students may be based on student record information, including test data, past grades, comments by previous teachers, knowledge about the family or initial contact with the student in the classroom. Studies also show contact with students leads to the formation of stable (and largely accurate) differential expectations within a few days after the school year begins.

The best information illustrates formation of expectations is normal. This in itself is inherently neither good nor bad. Keep in mind the accuracy of the expectations and whether or not they are flexible or more permanent. Inaccurate expectations will cause damage if teachers not only do not correct them but begin to base instructional decisions on them.

Expectations tend to be self-sustaining. They affect perception by causing teachers to be alert to what they expect and less likely to notice what they do not expect. They affect interpretation by causing teachers to interpret, and perhaps distort, what they see so it remains consistent with their expectations. Some expectations persist although the facts may prove them inaccurate or unrealistic.

EYE OPENER

For teachers: Do you read school records of your new classes before the school year begins? Why or why not? Have you formed expectations about students as a result? How accurate did you find your expectations?

TRY THIS

For teachers: At the end of the day, have students share a success they have experienced during the day. Have them also share something they've learned. Watch for those with low self-esteem and help them think of something they may not have perceived as a success or as a learning experience. Other students may be able to help as well. More confident students will more quickly recognize even small successes.

Variation: Award stickers or other small prizes to students who recognize others' successes.

Henry Levin, a Stanford University economist and educator, founded the Accelerated Schools Project in 1986 in the San Francisco area. He's been a school critic for many years.

Anytime you start to sort out kids, you eventually build categories with given assumptions. If you start off saying this child is at risk, you're saying this child is defective. So we send the child to the repair shop. The problem is, you'll never make the child whole when you stigmatize the child in every possible way. You make the child see he or she isn't as good as the others. And in the meantime, other kids are moving ahead. Once the child is in the repair shop, he or she will never be out of the repair shop.

TRY THIS

For teachers: Discuss how we each have our own gifts. Talk about what attributes can be considered gifts. What's special about the child is what he or she identifies like being kind, having the ability to draw or being good at jumping rope. Cut slips of paper and have students write their gift(s) on the paper. Wrap them up in decorative paper. They can be Mother's Day or Father's Day (or any holiday) gifts.

All parents of *special needs children* (another label used in education) are familiar with the I.E.P., or Individual Educational Plan. Each child and his or her parent meet with teachers, counselors, and staff to determine goals for the school year, how they are to be accomplished and what criterion will be used to determine whether or not they have been met. The truth is, every child should have an educational plan to address their strengths and areas of need. Kids with learning disabilities or other difficulties to overcome need a formal one, but every child is unique and would benefit from the amount of attention an I.E.P. yields. As parents, we can draw up our own plans with our kids—after all, we know them best—and work with teachers to implement them. A good classroom teacher will have input about your child and most are happy to work with parents toward achieving goals for their students.

TO THINK ABOUT

For teachers: Have you set, or helped to set, goals for your students? Even very young children should be encouraged to set small goals, such as learning to tie their shoes. Older children can offer insight into what they need to work on. If they don't, help guide them. Organization is always difficult (even for adults!) and can certainly be a goal for many middle- and high-school-aged students. Offer rewards as incentive. To an adult, the accomplishment of a goal is rewarding enough, but a new CD or trip to the movies can go a long way to offer encouragement to a child.

My son was having some problems with his fourth-grade teacher. He was talking a lot, talking without raising his hand, that kind of thing. Mostly it was because he's a bright kid and he just had a lot to share, but he still needed to work within the classroom rules. Otherwise with thirty kids, things can get crazy. The teacher and I talked. I told her my son worked better with a definite reward system for the "right" behavior rather than a punishment for the "wrong" behavior.

She was pleased I took the time to have a talk with her about it, was sensitive to the problem, and willing to work with her. We started a simple reward system. Ridiculously simple, but it worked. The best thing about it was the teacher and I figured it out together. She stopped being frustrated, and my son was able to gain some positive attention. But it wouldn't have happened if I hadn't been able to offer her the insight. You really have to take the time.

—Karen T.

Gifted is a label for which many parents would give a great deal to have applied to their child. However, raising a gifted child presents many challenges. Often these children are hyper-sensitive to their environment, to themselves, indeed, to life. Sometimes they need extra patience and understanding in dealing with ordinary events.

I've been teaching gifted children for many, many years, and it's never easy. It's always interesting, rewarding, and fun, but never easy. I remember one girl in particular, one of the most brilliant children I've ever been privileged to have in my class. One day her pencil case fell apart. And so did she. The way she reacted to this trivial little thing was way out of proportion. I tried to help her understand we could get her a new one, it wasn't such a major catastrophe, but she would have none of it. The thing is, I went to several seminars about gifted children, and I learned this type of reaction was right in the profile of this type of kid.

—Joan J.

Parents of gifted children need to communicate with them. They need to be intensely involved with the child's education, and know the child well enough to know when there are problems. They need to help their children find a range of challenges, not just academic ones.

Only the educated are free.
—Epictetus

The effects of teasing can be devastating to a child who does not have an adult who will listen and acknowledge the hurt. Oftentimes it may not be easily discernable who is doing the teasing and to what extent. Providing emotional support, demonstrating a willingness to take on serious offenders and at least contact the school will be reassuring to your child. They will know they have your complete support. Keep avenues for discussion open at all times.

It is the supreme art of the teacher to awaken joy in creative expression and knowledge.
—Albert Einstein

A teacher is better than two books.
—German Proverb

Some children are still labeled *gifted and talented* by means of an individual intelligence quotient (I.Q.) test, usually given in first grade. A child who achieves a score of 130 is given this distinction even though an I.Q. test is not the measure of a child's native intelligence, but the measure of a child's performance on that particular test. This score is not a permanent or unchangeable figure, despite popular belief. A child's motivation and ability to concentrate are only two of the variables that can change scores. Some districts will forever screen a child with a less-than-adequate score *out* of programs for gifted children. Others (and this number is continually increasing in number) recognize gaps created by testing will identify these children for inclusion in appropriate programs. It is puzzling that adults need an I. Q. test score in order to decide what a child can or cannot do.

The designation of gifted can be a burden and is potentially discouraging in families where one member is gifted or talented, while others are not. This labeling of our children sticks. They conform to our best and worst expectations.

At our school, we believe in not putting limits on what kids can accomplish. If one of our students, for example, decides they want to take an AP (advanced placement) class, and maybe they don't have the grades that would normally get them in there, we'll stand behind them and say, "Okay. If you feel like you're up to the challenge, we'll do everything we can to help you succeed." And that's just what we do. Lots of times kids get judged, they get labels thrown on them, and it seems almost impossible to escape those labels. We work very hard to get away from them. It can be amazing what you find underneath a label sometimes.

—Joan H.

Some children do very well on tests because they have learned textbook lessons well. They may also be adept at rote memorization, which will also serve them well in testing. There are other, equally talented children, who do not do as well on tests because they see another way of solving a problem. This way may be more creative but does not yield the textbook answer.

Mavericks and more straight-line thinkers should be rewarded and encouraged. Sometimes the maverick thinker is discouraged at school because only those who give textbook answers receive any recognition, including good grades. Luckily, most creative children continue with their creative ways in spite of what they are provided or denied by the schools. Adults can be most helpful to them by not standing in their way and providing them with the materials, the time, and the space they need to carry out their projects. Psychologist Teresa Amabile, of Brandeis University, studied creative people for nine years. She found, when people were inspired by their own interests and enjoyment, there was a better chance they would explore unlikely paths, take risks, and produce something unique and useful in the end.

> ### TRY THIS
>
> *For teachers:* Conduct a learning experiment in your classroom. Look for ways to pair disparate thinkers in a project or task. Put kids together who would not normally choose to collaborate. This experiment doesn't need to engage the whole class. Work with a few students at a time. Praise and encourage them to work together. Monitor their progress closely. The project or task should be involved enough that the students are spending time working together. When the project is complete, get feedback on how things went. Once you've had time to observe everyone, reveal your experiment to the class. What did they think worked, what did not, and why? Remind them to keep the discussion away from labeling and blaming. Discuss ways they we can work together with people they either don't know or don't have things in common with.

Dean Keith Simonton, a psychologist at the University of California, found very inventive people were in many ways quite ordinary. Many were lackluster pupils, neither especially well educated nor particularly brainy. Although creative people were intelligent, high I.Q. was no guarantee of success and sometimes too much education got in the way. The danger in education, he concluded, was picking up rote methods for doing things sometimes precluded more creative solutions.

Most students are more motivated by challenging learning environments. All students, having mastered the basic curriculum, should have the opportunity and be encouraged to engage in enrichment activities according to their talents and interests. Schools should avoid labeling children, which breeds self-fulfilling prophecies. Children whose self-worth is closely attached to the label of gifted and talented, may be afraid to take chances lest they be found-out to not be truly gifted. In extreme cases, they might stop trying for fear of failure. Getting less than perfect grades is often considered failure by very talented students. All children have the potential for being adept or skillful at some level in some area, and their potential deserves to be nourished, nurtured, and encouraged.

Educating young people is truly an awesome responsibility. It takes humor, insight, cooperation, and a little luck.

Chapter Five

Getting Personal

Life for both sexes is arduous, difficult, a perpetual struggle.
It calls for gigantic courage and strength.

—Virginia Wolff

Love and stoplights can be cruel.

—Sesame Street,
children's television show

A father and son were driving on the highway. The father lost control, swerved off the road and ran into a telephone pole. The father died instantly, and his son was critically injured.

An ambulance rushed the boy to a nearby hospital. When a prominent surgeon was called to provide immediate treatment a gasp was heard. "I can't operate on this boy," the surgeon said, "He's my son." How can that be? The answer: the surgeon was the boy's mother.

Because we spend so much time at work, being labeled there can significantly affect our lives, particularly if we think of men and women with regard to specific roles and behaviors. A woman's role is thought to be passive, tactful, assistive, and emotional, whereas men are stereotyped as aggressive, tough, independent, and unemotional. In short, as the story above implies, women are not supposed to be surgeons.

EYE OPENER

What is the worst scenario of sexual stereotyping you've experienced? Have you ever judged anyone by a stereotype? How have your attitudes changed since you were a teenager?

As long as there have been people, there have been labels and stereotypes about men and women. As much as there is to unite us, there's just as much to divide us. If relationships between the sexes aren't solid and mutually respectful, there is ample opportunity for labeling. Resulting misunderstandings vary from the funny to the fatal. In fact, the very subject provides so much material for discussion, this entire chapter is devoted to it.

Men and women have spent history attributing behaviors, abilities, interests, values, and roles to a person or group on the basis of gender. Females are weak, males are strong...on and on it goes, except most of us are no longer content to accept that kind of labeling. Like most labeling, it's too restrictive. This type of labeling, firmly embedded in our (Western) cultural heritage, certainly warrants some exploration. Thankfully, over time we are seeing a definite sense of change.

TRY THIS

For older students: Work as a class or in smaller discussion groups. What do you think are the worst preconceptions girls have about boys and boys have about girls? Is there truth to any of them? What are masculine traits? Which traits are feminine? Can you define any gender-neutral traits? Encourage open discussion without engaging in a battle of the sexes.

I love her and she loves me, and we hate each other with a wild hatred born of love.

—August Strindberg

Gender issues have long been favorites with sociological researchers. One study investigated the impact of target age on gender stereotyping. It examined how gender-stereotypical traits varied from adults to children. Children ages eight to ten and adults viewed photographs of men, women, boys, and girls (referred to as "targets"). They rated each pictured individual on the possession of masculine, feminine, and gender-neutral personality traits.

Adults and children showed evidence of gender stereotyping. The strongest level of stereotyping was seen when adults rated child targets. They were particularly unwilling to attribute feminine characteristics to young males. Participants of both ages viewed adult targets, regardless of sex, as more masculine and less feminine than child targets. Adult participants rated traditionally masculine and feminine traits on the likelihood of possession by adults versus children. Feminine traits were believed to be more childlike and less adult-like than masculine traits. By middle childhood, children typically have acquired extensive, adult-like knowledge about gender stereotyping of personality traits. They know which are *girl things* and *boy things*. It's hard to deter them once they've acquired this set of rules.

When our first child was born, we wanted to ensure we were not buying gender stereotyped toys. Our first child was a girl. She never seemed to care too much about "girl stuff," preferring a varied assortment of toys. Dolls and stuffed animals, she pretty much ignored. When our son was born, we went to a store that specialized in toys and clothing for very young children and we bought our son a "doll" that felt more like a stuffed animal. Our boy wanted nothing to do with it. It was funny. All he wanted were things with wheels. He just pushed the doll away and said "truck" over and over. Truck meant trucks, cars, wagons—anything with wheels, that's what he would play with. He didn't want anything to do with the doll or stuffed animals. All he wanted was what you might call "boy toys." This happened before he was old enough to pay too much attention to TV, so I know it wasn't media influenced. I'm still not sure about what all that means, but I do know my son was what people used to call "all boy" right from the start.

—Mark B.

The implicit assumption in these studies is, stereotypes apply equally to children and adults. There is reason to suspect that target age may influence when stereotypes become active. Maybe people believe children, still learning about gender roles in our society, are less sex-differentiated than adults. This would suggest stereotyping should be more extensive when people are judging adult targets than when judging child targets.

TRY THIS

For younger learners: Ask young children to define love. As often as you might think this is done, it is still a revealing exercise. As a teacher, you can gain wonderful insights into your students. If you use the answers to decorate gifts for parents, they will have something they can treasure always. If the answers are compiled into a class book, you create a very touching, and often astute, reflection of the adult world through the eyes of the child.

Impressions about stereotypes may become more flexible with age. It is believed children who seem rigidly bound by stereotypes, more so than adults, have not yet developed their flexible, individualized personalities. This view implies stereotyping should be more extensive when people are judging child targets than when they are judging adult targets, and adults should engage in less stereotyping than children do.

Among those whom I like or admire, I can find no common denominator, but among those whom I love, I can: all of them make me laugh.

—W. H. Auden

Along with gender bias let's discuss sexual harassment, which has been called the "older cousin to bullying." The American Association of University Women (AAUW) conducted a landmark survey of 1,632 students in grades eight to eleven. An astonishing 85 percent of girls and 76 percent of boys reported experiencing some kind of harassment. The milder forms included looks, jokes, graffiti on bathroom walls, and comments about body parts. The more severe forms were physically intrusive; being grabbed or brushed up against in a sexual way. Thirty-one percent of the girls experienced harassment "often," compared to only 18 percent of the boys. Thirteen percent of the girls and 9 percent of the boys reported being "forced to do something sexual at school other than kissing."

I thought I'd heard just about everything until the day my fourth-grade daughter came home telling me about girls trying to get boys to "ask them out," and some of the other girls who were talking about boyfriends. The boys were just as bad, talking about girls they were trying to ask out—the usual high school stuff about the popular girls being much more difficult to ask out, of course.

When did they get to be in such a big hurry? These kids are eight and nine years old! Why do their parents allow such nonsense? Fortunately my daughter was a throwback to earlier times and thought such stuff was really "icky." It's a good thing, too. I told both of my kids they were much too young to be thinking about such things. "Boyfriend," "girlfriend"— they don't need labels like this so young. I know adults who can't handle those labels.

—Barb C.

This is my first year in high school. I was going to join a service club, because I was in one in middle school and I really liked it. The one I was going to join had boys and girls in it. That was okay, but when I found a club that was all girls, I picked that one instead. Right now, it's just easier to not have to worry about boys being there. It would make me nervous. My mom was teasing me, and she said by the time I was a junior I would be joining the other club. She's probably right, and I agreed with her. By then I'll be adjusted to high school, more comfortable being in that environment. Right now, I just like being with other girls in my club. We have fun, we do some really good projects, and we don't have to worry about how we look and how we act and stuff like that, which we would do if boys were there. I know that's not what we're supposed to be thinking about when we're doing service projects and stuff, but you can't help it.

—Kara Y.

Concerns like these are one reason for the recent resurgence of same-sex education. In California, some school districts are experimenting with same-sex academies with great success. Both genders reported a greater sense of freedom in expressing their ideas and interacting with each other in everyday situations. In one informal survey, all but one seventh-grade girl said they would make the same choice again and half of the boys said they would. Nothing can completely ensure gender equity in education. It is an option parents can use, if available and if they think it will benefit their child. Knowing your child well is critical.

There are many steps we can take in an effort to minimize gender bias and sexual harassment.

As a woman, you can talk openly about sex, and keep talking as you get deeper into a relationship. Be careful not to let alcohol or other drugs decrease your ability to take care of yourself and make sensible decisions. Trust your gut feelings. If a place or the way a person acts makes you nervous or uneasy, get out. Check out a first date or a blind date with friends. Insist on going to a public place like a movie, sporting event or restaurant. Carry money for a phone call and taxi or take your own car. Don't leave a party, concert, game, or other social occasion with someone you just met or don't know well. Be conscientious of people you associate yourself with, particularly anyone who puts you down or tries to control the way you dress or your choice of friends.

Men, ask yourselves how sexual stereotypes affect your attitudes and actions toward relationships. Don't interpret the answer "no" as a challenge, accept it as a final decision. Avoid clouding your judgment with alcohol or drugs. Understand forcing someone to have sex against their will is rape, a violent crime with serious consequences. Never be drawn into a gang rape...at parties, fraternities, bars, or after sporting events. Seek counseling or a support group to help you deal with any feelings of violence or aggression.

TO THINK ABOUT

What else can you do?

- Monitor the media for programs or videos that reinforce sexual stereotypes. Write or call to protest. On the other side, publicly commend the media when they highlight the realities of date rape.
- Ask college or professional athletes (or other role models) to talk with high school students about sexual stereotyping and responsible behavior.
- Ask your church or civic group to organize a speaker and panel discussion on the theme, "Please Listen to Me—How Men and Women Talk to Each Other."

TRY THIS

For middle school students: Would you like to see same-sex academies for students at your school? In your district? Why or why not? What do you think would be the biggest difference, aside from the absence of boys or girls, in how school was conducted? Make a list of all the pros and cons. Debate the issue.

Inappropriate behavior had a more significant impact on girls. A greater percentage of the female students described feeling less confident, more self-conscious, shamed, and embarrassed. Young women can be so affected by harassment their grades drop. In the AAUW survey, one in four girls said they stayed home from school or cut class because of sexual harassment.

The first time I experienced sexual harassment, I didn't even realize that's what it was, much less what it was called. I was eighteen, very inexperienced, and quite shy. It would never have occurred to me my boss would think of me in a sexual way. Fortunately, he didn't start out bothering me when I went to work there. It was a summer job and I really needed the money. At first everything was fine. I worked for a couple who owned a dry-cleaning business. At first I dealt just with her, or with both of them. Over the course of the summer, it seemed like it started to be just him. It sounds like it came out of a movie, but it's true.

At last this guy decided he was going to make a move on me. Every night when we closed, we'd take care of all the business, counting the drawer, receipts, all that stuff. There would be cleaning to sort out, other cleaning that had come in from the plant where they did the work. They had the mechanized thing that had all the clean clothing on it. That night he starts pursuing me around this thing while we're hanging up clothes. The first thing he did was put his hands on me. At this point, so long ago, I don't really remember all the details. But chasing somebody around moving clothing, that you don't forget.

I was too embarrassed to tell anybody, even my parents. That just goes to show you what the climate was like then. Nobody talked about sexual harassment. I don't think it happened any less, but it wasn't a common topic of conversation like it is now. It was years before I ever talked about this to anyone, before I recognized it for what it was. I just felt lucky, at the time, that the summer was almost over before he started. It made me feel just awful, and I didn't know what to do. I felt like I had nobody to talk to. I knew if I said anything to my parents they'd make me quit, and I couldn't afford that. My father was a quiet kind of guy, but if he'd known about that, the stuff would have hit the fan.

—Georgia B.

TO THINK ABOUT

Where did the idea of pink for girls and blue for boys originate? Are those the colors you'll want when you're ready to have a family? Were they the colors your parents used for your baby things? What other colors would be good? Can boys and girls use the same colors? Why or why not?

TRY THIS

For older students: Develop a list of characteristics and behaviors. Decide whether they're feminine (pink) or masculine (blue). The purpose of this activity is to increase awareness of thoughts, feelings, beliefs, and behaviors related to gender identity, gender roles, and sexual orientation. An important point is to listen to and understand the attitudes and feelings of others. Students should also strive to become more discerning of the ways institutions and cultures address gender issues. Working through these kinds of discussions, they will come to feel affirmed in their own identities.

Sex, or gender, bias is defined as "behavior resulting from the assumption one sex is superior to the other." Gender bias has become an important topic for writers of all disciplines. Gender bias is another way of labeling roles and situations as masculine or feminine. This enables, however subtly, a continuation of the idea that particular jobs belong to one gender rather than the other. Example: "When the CEO of the company speaks, he demands attention" can be replaced with, "When speaking, the CEO of the company demands attention."

Love does not consist of gazing at each other, but in looking together in the same direction.

—Antoine de Saint-Exupery

When we had to change health plans, I was finally able to choose a pediatrician, not just take one assigned by my plan. I chose a woman. The male physician we'd been dealing with was excellent, and had always given us great care, but I had another concern, which was for me equally important, given that our new doctor was also someone we felt comfortable dealing with. My then husband was revealing a chauvinist streak a mile wide. He would make snide comments about women; he would make immature jokes about male nurses…lots more inappropriate remarks. I felt very strongly I needed to help send a message to my children that women could be physicians. It's not the kind of behavior I would normally choose. It felt a bit out of character when I analyzed my motives, later, but in retrospect, it was absolutely the right thing to do.

—Blanca M.

Bias can distract readers from the topic about which you are trying to inform them. Use of the term "man" to denote all people is a common occurrence, although as a society we are becoming increasingly sensitive to it. The fix can be relatively simple. "For centuries, men have struggled to find the meaning of life" becomes "For centuries, *people* have struggled to find the meaning of life." Another example, "Whenever a professor assigns a paper, he insists on correct grammar," implies all professors are men. English does not have a gender-neutral, singular pronoun for use when referring to people. Often, a writer will then resort to writing "When a professor assigns a paper, he or she insists on correct grammar," or sometimes, "he/she insists on correct grammar." Another possibility is the s/he construction, although some writers loathe this form. Some writers alternate he with she, stating in an opening paragraph the intent to do so.

These awkward sentences are most easily avoided by converting the noun to its plural form and rewriting the sentence accordingly. "Whenever professors assign a paper, they insist on correct grammar." Although the prevailing thought might be awareness in the area of women's rights, let's not forget the sword cuts both ways. "A nurse must strive to make her patient comfortable," is better stated, "Nurses must strive to make their patients comfortable."

Language is a big culprit for perpetuating gender bias. Although expressions like "person-hole cover" or "jury foreperson" might sound odd, words in the vernacular for any length of time become common-place. Change is often upsetting to one degree or another. And maybe the words *are* funny. A sense of humor helps.

He who falls in love with himself will have no rivals.

—Benjamin Franklin

TRY THIS

List as many gender-biased words as you can, including ones for which gender-neutral alternatives have been created. Devise alternatives of your own.

Although adults can learn to determine which expectations are real and which are not, this is not necessarily so for children. They can absorb expectations without awareness. Computers are a prominent example. A study by a British research team suggests boys are not inherently better at using computers, but those preconceptions and the male qualities of the software negatively affect girls' performance. Studies of UK school pupils at all age levels typically reveal noteworthy gender differences in attitudes to computing. Boys are usually more positive—which runs counter to the overall performance of girls, who usually do better than boys. When girls and boys worked together in teams on the computer, they did equally well. When they worked next to each other on separate machines, however, the boys did much better than the girls. This was true at the time and in subsequent individual tests.

One aspect of the study suggested the language of the computer activities themselves was contributory to these results. When the children were asked to solve a reasoning problem in the form of an adventure game involving kings, pirates, and mechanical forms of transportation such as ships and planes, the boys did significantly better than the girls. When the characters in the game were honey bears and the transportation included a pony and a balloon, the gender difference totally disappeared. The boys did slightly worse than in the previous game, but the girls' performance improved almost twofold and they did a little better than the boys.

Once again, the specter of self-fulfilling prophecy seems to be at work. The study also seemed to suggest the children themselves expect boys to be better with computers, so they are.

EYE OPENER

For adults: Is there anything in your work environment that resembles the situation in the study above? Are there remedies available to change the situation? Is your workplace a gender-neutral model?

For older learners: Are there any programs or situations at your school you feel are gender-biased? How do these things make you feel? Do you have any suggestions to change this?

TRY THIS

Inventory your computer games and other activities. How many of them are what might be classified as "boys work"? How many are aimed specifically at girls? Are there any changes you can make to achieve an even blend if you don't have one now?

Take it further for older learners. Split the class into teams of game designers. Group students by gender. The challenge will be to make the main character in the game the opposite of that of the group. Try the activity with mixed groups. For the students, the object is game design. For the teacher, it's twofold. . . to observe differences in how the groups interact and the find out what roles the divided genders come up with for their opposite-gender characters. Do you observe significant differences? Use the different kinds of groups as a springboard for discussion of gender differences and roles. Ask students if there was any labeling going on within their groups.

According to Bournemouth University Professor Paul Light, "It's thought performances are a product of gender expectations about computer-related abilities. If girls expect boys are going to be better with computers, or if boys think they should be better than girls, then the absence of any actual interaction may allow these expectations to become self-fulfilling prophesies." He says, although there's no evidence of real gender differences, girls may often approach computer tasks with lower expectations of success than boys.

Computers are so vital in all aspects of life, it's clear we must validate and encourage girls until such a time as there is parity in expectations. Attitudes change slowly, but they can change.

TRY THIS

When discussing how attitudes change, people will often say how extreme they feel attitudes are. Fashion a pendulum and observe the wide arcs it makes. Discuss how often, in order to change, attitudes start at one end of the arc and then swing to the other before they settle down in the middle.

I hated having to call tech support when I purchased a new computer. The techs invariably were male, and just as invariably when they heard a female voice on the other end of the line, they would assume I knew absolutely nothing.

I was having problems with my printer and couldn't resolve them, so I had to call. Before I did, I tried the usual routine of options, which, by the way, were the same things a male friend of mine tried when I asked him if he could figure out what was wrong. So, I was stuck. I called. First, he goes into his "It's a woman so use your special voice" mode. Then, one by one he went down the list of options I had tried. As we went down the list, the tone of his voice changed. Inside, I was laughing. I laughed even harder when he had to put me on hold and ask his supervisor because the things he tried didn't work either. By the time he got back, he was respectful.

—Helen A.

TO THINK ABOUT

Create a definition of gender equity.

Equal education free from discrimination based on sex. It means helping students free themselves from limited, rigid, sex-role stereotypes, and sex bias. It means students will understand, think about, and prepare for a future characterized by change, especially in male and female life roles, relationships, and careers.

—Sheboygan Area School
District Policy, 1991

It didn't take long after we were married before he started calling me all kinds of names. "Stupid" was one of his favorites. He was sneaky about it, almost always he disguised his games in the form of a joke. But after a while, even teasing can go too far. And yeah, it's one thing to know you're not what somebody's calling you. I think somewhere deep down I started to absorb it like it was true. I always thought of myself as pretty strong. Guess I wasn't strong enough. Or I didn't want to see what was really going on, or to try and deal with it, because there was no dealing with it.

—Tricia F.

It is better to be hated for what you are than to be loved for what you are not.

—Andre Gide

I had orders that kept me away from home for a year. A buddy asked me if that caused problems. Earlier in my life, I would have thought that was a really stupid question, but by that point, I had enough experience to know better. All my ideas about what a marriage was and what a family was, that was all shot. By then I had come to realize once she had her kids and my check coming in, she had all she needed. I was just something that got in her way or that she had to put up with when I was around. I missed my kids, though. Lots of people like to pretend it's not as important for a man to be there as it is for the mother, but it's not that way with me, or with lots of the men I know. I think so many times the deck is stacked against men when it comes to divorce. Why is it a woman should automatically get custody? I always took much better care of the kids than she did, and I barely get to see them.

—David S.

With the right preparation and some amount of maturity, relationships can also be an equally fertile ground for growth and development. Information is a powerful tool. Having the information about what a particular relationship is will empower us to take care of ourselves in it. That means understanding ourselves, our partners, and our ideas about boundaries and how they fit into a relationship. Taking care of ourselves in a relationship by setting boundaries may seem selfish. As a song says, "It ain't necessarily so."

Are you guilty of sexual stereotyping? What labels do you throw out without thinking? If you do, is it done in jest?

Setting boundaries is one of the most important steps in creating a healthy, loving, and respectful relationship. Boundaries are crucial in helping a couple define and maintain their unique personality and in defining how they impact the outside world. Will the impact be positive? Will the world see you as a unified force, with each other and the relationship coming first? Or do you exhibit permeable boundaries in which there are passive-aggressive interactions, designed to publicly express your ongoing frustrations—frustrations you have not learned to air constructively and meaningfully at home?

The struggle for power and the issue of control have defined many relationships. They've also sounded the death knell for many relationships. When control identifies a relationship, independence and privacy are shut down, even feared. "Control freak" is an often-heard label.

Control sets up a system of dependency and co-dependency. Someone with a need for control thinks they're protecting themselves from abandonment. It doesn't work that way. Fear becomes the focus of life. It pushes your partner further away, even if they're right there. Remember the pop song that begins *"One is the loneliest number."* The next line is even more telling when it comes to relationships *"Two can be as bad as one, the loneliest number since the number one."* The more insecure someone is, the more they try to control. It affords a measure of peace, but it's a short-term fix for many relationships. "Co-dependent," although an accurate representation of behavior, can itself become a label too easily tossed out with no accompanying resolution to change.

I used to say I didn't know why I stayed so long, but that wasn't true. Well maybe it was, at the time. Truth is, I didn't have a whole lot of insight about why I stayed. Either that or I just didn't want to admit it. I was afraid. I was afraid of lots of things, him included, by the time it was over because he got really dangerous at times.

My self-esteem was so low it was off the radar screen, but I really hated talking about what I considered pop psychology stuff. I thought it was silly, and that it didn't apply to me. Wrong. I was a textbook case. I even took pride in my "ability to survive" until the time came when surviving wasn't enough. I don't know what the defining moment was. It doesn't matter; it happened and I'm glad.

Some people told me I finally grew a backbone, but it wasn't quite that simple or so neat a package. Few things are, and it's no good trying to simplify things all the time. I recognize a lot of patterns in his behavior that I got used to in my growing up years. Some people are easier led than others, and I was one and didn't know it. In the areas of my life where I felt secure, I wouldn't dream of letting anybody push me around like that. Too bad it took so long to find that security and that strength, but at least it was there. I got insight. Better late than never.

—Dorothy P.

I used "co-dependent" as the biggest smokescreen around. It worked, for a while. Reading about that style of behavior gave me some insights as to why I stayed in a destructive marriage. The problem was, I stopped there, at least for a while. It was like sticking a Post-it Note on myself that said, "co-dependent." The label gave me an excuse to just stop in mid-correction. Labels have their uses, but I think that usefulness has definite boundaries. Then you have to keep expanding those boundaries. If you do that, labels won't fit, and that's the best, I think.

—Dana F.

With some, it's compulsion. It's "love me, but keep me from feeling my feelings," and, "if I can maintain turmoil, I will not remember my hurtful past." Compulsive love—love that is an addiction—results in disappointment, resentment, and frustration. Have you been there, done that? As long as you depend on someone outside yourself to make you feel comfortable in your own skin, you'll continue the pattern of self-destruction and emotional withdrawal and pain. Begin the process of believing you are whole within yourself.

I never understood the addictive personality until I got married. Love is blind? You know it. She was so needy all the time. I thought I liked that clingy stuff until I discovered she could never let go, never let me out of her sight. She was so jealous over nothing. I have my faults, but infidelity wasn't one of them. I could never convince her, though. She was emotionally arrested at somewhere about six years old, I swear. I tried to reassure her, but over time, her complaints about being hurt before and how she didn't want to have to bear it from me, too, just got to be too much. That kind of garbage just drove me away. I couldn't deal with it any more.

—Tom Y.

TRY THIS

Ask yourself: Who are some people who care for me? How do they show it? Who are the people I care about? Do I show them I care? If you do this exercise with a class, talk about the different kinds of people in their lives who can care for them. Talk about the many ways we can show each other we care.

If you're over voting age, you will probably have heard several excuses, statements, declarations, and old sayings about relationships. Popular among them may be, "I don't want to get hurt again." We trot that out to avoid doing any real work in a relationship. Until scientists find and clone the perfect human being, chances are somewhere along the line you'll be involved in a relationship and you'll get hurt. You may even hurt someone else. Intentional or not, it happens. It's up to each of us as to what to do with that hurt. We can use every barb to form new and higher walls around us. We can also break up the walls and use the pieces for kindling to start the fire of another, better relationship.

TRY THIS

List three of your own personality traits you don't like and explain why. Are they labels, like *neat freak*? Turn those labels into something positive like *well organized*. Now, list three events you thought were roadblocks in your life whether small or large. Find the good that came from them. Did you lose a job and find a better one? Maybe the pharmacist didn't have your prescription, but on the way out of the drugstore you found a perfect gift

(continued)

111

for a child who needs cheering up. The point is to learn to think the things working against us as more challenging ways of getting to the things we have going for us.

Finally, list five achievements of which you are particularly proud. Why? Because we often do not take the time to toot our own horns. Make another list of three things about yourself you'd like to improve. Striving juices up life. Complacency kills it. What three things do you take for granted? What five things would you next like to accomplish?

There is no sincerer love than the love of food.

—George Bernard Shaw (1856–1950)

TRY THIS

Use an online source or your local newspaper. Read the personal ads. Look for labels. *Athletic, slim, perky, generous,* and *handsome* are just a few. Write an ad for yourself—not necessarily for posting—but as a means of identifying yourself as a potential relationship partner. Do this even if you're in a relationship. It will tell you a lot about yourself.

Take it further for fun. . . write the silliest, funniest ad you can. Exaggerate all the characteristics you're looking for in a romantic relationship. Describe yourself in terms of your "alien pod" and where it's located.

It's no mystery: Men and women are different. This has been a source of endless confusion and amusement to both genders. Although there's been some improvement in communication, it seems like every generation has to make the same discoveries. One of the biggest differences is in communication style. Women, for the most part, like to share feelings. If they're happy, they call their friends to share their joy. If they're heartbroken, they call their friends to commiserate. They talk about their work and all the annoying things going on there, their families, and all the annoying things going on there and the great things the kids are doing along with the things that will bring them to gray hair sooner. They call to find out the same things that are going on with their friends. They just call. It's one of the most difficult things women don't understand about men: they *don't* talk and they don't call.

One word frees us of all the weight and pain of life: that word is love.
—Sophocles

It didn't take long in our marriage before I started hearing the name-calling. I don't know what hurt more, the names or the fact he started calling me things he'd never even hinted at before we got married. It was such an about-face it was scary, like I had never known this guy before. He didn't do it every day. Like many abusers, his idea was if I wasn't black and blue—physically or emotionally—then I had no cause for complaint. They all say that. It's supposed to make you feel better or something, as though you're imagining what they're doing and stop whining already.

It doesn't work that way. Somebody beats you up, either with their fists or their mouth, it's still getting beat up. Don't try and make excuses for your behavior. It's just wrong. It wasn't the same thing as losing your temper once in a while, either. He tried to tell me that one. At first it was supposed to be jokes, but it never felt like that. I was never sold that bill of goods, but I tried very hard. Who wants to think they've just made the biggest possible mistake of their lives? Not me, especially when people have warned you that you're walking into something that's going to turn out badly.

—Bianca T.

If men do call, it's not to share feelings. It's to discuss a computer problem, a car problem or maybe a business problem. If they call, while they're on the phone they might pass along a joke or engage in some one-upmanship. They do *not* call to discuss their relationships, families or jobs unless they're trying to hit up their friends for job leads. How often have you heard men insult each other by referring to each other as *ladies*?

It is most unwise for people in love to marry.
—Ralph Waldo Emerson

The problem, of course, is these two styles are so disparate a clash is inevitable. Women are offended when a man they're involved with doesn't call to chat. A woman communicates "I care about you," by staying in touch often. They will even call just to say "Hi. I was thinking about you." A man calls when he has something specific in mind to tell her, for example, or if he wants to ask a woman out for an evening. To a man, a call about nothing is confusing and sometimes annoying. To a woman, *not* getting a call about nothing is neglectful and inconsiderate. It says to her the man is not thinking about her at all when, in fact, he may have been thinking a great deal about her. He may even have dropped your name over a cup of coffee with a buddy. The woman needs to recognize the lack of constant communication does not mean "I'm gonna dump her." The man needs to know the occasional phone call just to say hello, though it may seem like the emotional Mount Everest to him is the "my hero" to her. These behaviors often lead to the use of two frequently used labels: men calling women illogical and women referring to men as insensitive.

TRY THIS

Write six sentences beginning with "I love...." How many sentences involved people or even pets? How many involved something else, say food, for example? Do you really *love* your food? Talk about the use of the word, and how it has come to be so diluted as to be almost meaningless in some circumstances.

TRY THIS

For high school students: Do some role play about phone calls. Try switching gender roles. Boys create skits involving girls calling each other and girls create scenarios in which boys call each other. Discuss the results. How accurate were the representations?

TRY THIS

For teachers: Ask students to draw pictures of how they think they'll look when they are adults.

Where do our notions of romance originate? The proliferation of print and online media having to do with relationships is astonishing. What would have been unthinkable a few generations ago is commonplace today. Popular music is rife with young men and women singing lyrics that leave little to the imagination, and the lyrics are becoming the popular literature of our day, passed on to younger and younger audiences. Magazines targeted at teenage girls regularly feature articles whose headlines draw in their young readers with promises on delivering dating tips and advice on how to recognize who is the *right one*. Here, too, labeling is rife. Any magazine cover will yield bounty like *hottie* or *dream guy*. Any teenager can tell you what the labels mean and how important they are. They know, too, what the infamous *popular* means.

TRY THIS

For older students: Create a list of labels tossed around in students' casual conversation. Discuss what they mean. Are they meant to denigrate? Do they?

TRY THIS

For older students and adults: How have notions of romance changed in popular culture, such as movies? Select scenes from movies of the 1950s through the 1990s. What are the similarities and differences? Are today's movies any more or less truthful about reflecting relationships between men and women? Why or why not? If you were making a movie that involved a romantic relationship, what would that movie be?

Some labels gain popularity or prestige over time. Prime among them is *feminist*. When the feminist movement was in its infancy, it was a term with radical connotations. Today men and women use it freely—and with respect.

There's another label associated with relationships, although it's more accurately used to describe merely being unmarried: single. In some circles, it appears to be a bad word. With some friends, it appears to be a battle cry to fix you up with somebody, whether you want that service or not. For women in particular it can be a label that denotes anything from a shrewish personality to a physique that wouldn't attract a man who'd been in prison for twenty years. For a man it can mean an automatic assumption he's gay.

Most singles Internet sources are determined to fix your problem of being single. There are relationship coaches and dating coaches who help you get into relationships and still others who commiserate with you when a relationship breaks up. Is it beyond common understanding that some people might just prefer a single life? At least one fictional

character handles that very well. Kinsey Milhone expresses her satis-
faction with her single (after two divorces) status in each novel.

*Anyone who knows me will tell you that I cherish my unmarried
state.*

—Sue Grafton's female private investigator
character, *Kinsey Milhone*, in *E is for Evidence*

TRY THIS

For singles: Have you ever been fixed up with a date? Have you ever told your friends to kindly stop fixing you up? Is being single a concern for you, or are you satisfied with that aspect of your life.

For Couples: Are you among those who cannot resist trying to find that special someone for all your single friends? Are you of the belief that unattached adults are always lonely and looking for companionship?

What's most important to consider regarding the single lifestyle is to respect the right of each person to determine whether or not they need or want a significant other. As the divorce rate will testify, not everybody is cut out for marriage. In this more enlightened state, it ought to be perfectly acceptable to go out to eat, go to a movie or any other venue and not have people stare because we're alone. *Single* is another label we need to be aware of.

Chapter Six

Hi, Society!

Love and work are the cornerstones of our humanness.
—Sigmund Freud

The Two Crabs

One beautiful day two crabs came out from their home to take a stroll on the sand.

"My child," said the mother, "you are walking very ungracefully. You should train yourself to walk straight forward without twisting from side to side."

"Then mother," said the young one, "if you set the example yourself, I will follow you and walk just as you do."

Example is the best teaching.

In this chapter we'll explore other aspects of our lives where we find labeling, from the doctor's office to the schoolroom. Just as labeling is a fact of life in the school environment, levels of education (or lack of them) can also give rise to labeling born of snobbery and humility:

My father-in-law had to drop out of school at about eighth grade to help support his family. That's what people did then. He never got over it, despite the success he had as an adult. He later owned two businesses, both of which did very well. In his second business he dealt with a variety of goods, but one thing he really enjoyed was

117

selling antiques. He educated himself about this over the course of his lifetime, and was in fact quite well read. He always researched the more unusual items that came his way in the course of his business. That was one of the things he enjoyed the most.

He certainly was knowledgeable about American history in particular. But like many self-educated people, he was never comfortable with that. He always felt keenly the lack of his formal education. "College boy" was something he liked to throw out all the time. The fact that he knew more than many people with a great deal more formal education was, in and of itself, not enough to fill that void he felt. Like some others, too, it caused him to become defensive. He was fond of putting down people with college degrees, including his son.

—Laurie H.

Earlier in history, just being able to do a job was often sufficient for getting and keeping it. It's much harder now to do the same thing without benefit of a college degree. Employers will often seek "the paper" for a variety of reasons, none of which has a direct bearing on an individual's ability to perform the tasks required. It's a situation bound to generate problems for some people.

I got more and more frustrated on my job as I was asked to do more and more, and received no additional help—or money. I developed two databases to handle the workload. It really streamlined all the data I was asked to manage. I did it on my own, without any training, because they weren't offering to send me to any classes or anything. But that's not what bothered me nearly so much as the fact two different people got promoted over me because they had college degrees. One had been there barely six months before getting promoted. I'd been on the job two years, but because I just had my associate's degree—I didn't get the promotion.

—Lisa M.

Some like to use their accomplishments in education as a social club to humiliate others around them, as Donna L. found out:

Hi, Society!

One of my jobs while working my way through college was in a deli. We had a big lunch trade, and since we were in the heart of a downtown business district we attracted a varied clientele that included lawyers, sometimes judges, secretaries, and other professional people. One day when we were particularly busy, a couple was waiting in line for a few minutes to place their order. Maybe they were just cranky, I don't know, but they started talking in loud voices and using arcane language to show off. They were being obnoxious, but what I really remember about them was some word they made a point of saying "Oh, she'll never know what that means," and making a point that I heard that.

Why bother? As it happened, I didn't know the word, but that wasn't important. I was a university student; I would have looked it up. I was an accomplished student, a good musician, and a future teacher with other distinct talents. But they made me feel stupid. I know you can't make anybody feel any way without giving them permission, but at the time I was really young and hadn't developed much self-confidence. Those affirmations work if you believe in them. Those people just wanted to show off, to humiliate me. They made me mad. It was a good thing we were busy, and I didn't have time to tell them off. Normally I wouldn't do that; for one thing I know if I didn't get fired, I would at least get in trouble. At the time, I would have been glad to be fired. Snobs like that don't get any real value from their education. Instead of passing along and sharing they just posture. It's empty and pointless. Without saying it, they slapped a "stupid waitress" label on me and had me all figured out because of it. You can label people by your actions as much as by your words.

TRY THIS

Share something about which you have special knowledge. Have a day where students in your class share something special they know and can pass along. For younger children it can be something as simple as tying their shoes. This might be a great way to organize a tutoring program. Upper grade children love helping lower grade kids. Everybody wins. You can do this in a church setting, too, or in your own neighborhood. Somebody somewhere can benefit from something you know. There's bound to be people around you, too, who would love to share something they know.

Recent Supreme Court decisions have made employers account-able for all forms of sexual harassment, regardless of whether or not it is reported by an employee. This includes harassment of male employees. All forms should be taken seriously and claims followed through, re-gardless of the gender of the employee filing the grievance.

One of the biggest issues posing an obvious barrier to easing sexual harassment is women's reluctance to label and report incidents of sexual harassment. This failure to identify and report has been termed the "silent reaction to sexual harassment syndrome." It may serve to per-petuate the existence of sexual harassment. The under reporting of sexual harassment has been well documented. Several large-scale stud-ies have indicated only a small number of victims seek any type of formal method of dealing with the problem. The majority of sexual harass-ment victims are likely to ignore the behaviors even though they generally see this strategy as ineffective. Why? Those who report any type of misconduct are always vulnerable to the inevitable name-call-ing and labeling that can be a consequence of trying to right wrongs, anything from *whistle blower* (although popular usage tends to give this term a favorable connotation) to the more objectionable slang terms men have for women.

One reason for the reluctance to report sexual harassment may be women believe formal reporting will not be useful or helpful to them. In a 1988 study, 50 percent of federal employees who had been ha-rassed reported the perpetrator to their supervisors, but less than half of those individuals reported this strategy was effective in resolving the situation. In addition, studies of women in organizational contexts have found they do not believe their reports will be handled adequately and effectively. Many also believe reporting may lead to, or be associated with, job termination. Other factors thought to influence a victim's likelihood of reporting sexual harassment include the severity of the offense, feminist ideology and gender-role attitudes about self-esteem and gender bias in sexual harassment policies. Girls who are raised with a strong sense of their own identities, and who are aware of the history of workplace bias against women will become working women aware of their right to a harassment-free workplace.

One theory about women's hesitancy to report harassment has cen-tered on the notion women often do not choose to use the sexual harassment label, and consequently do not report the behavior to a legitimate authority. The labeling of harassment itself may have an important relationship to the ultimate decision of whether or not to report. Many studies have demonstrated a reluctance on the part of women to apply the sexual harassment label. Although women often admit to experiencing a good deal of what researchers would label sexual harassment, women themselves do not label them as such.

EYE OPENER

What are the policies regarding sexual harassment in your workplace? Are they designed to pre-empt sexual harassment or merely deal with it should it occur? When were they put in place? Do you consider them adequate? If not, do you have any ideas as to how to make them more effective?

One survey showed 60 percent of women in a sample of faculty and graduate students said they had experienced what would qualify as sexual harassment. Less than 10 percent *reported* that they had been sexually harassed. Although over half their sample of women had experienced some form of sexual harassment, only 10 percent reported it with the sexual harassment label. Additionally, even women who perceive an incident as sexual harassment may not call it that. One study found, although only 3 percent of female participants used the label in response to an open-ended question, 98 percent of them agreed, when asked directly whether a specific act constituted sexual harassment. The gap between what really happens and what gets reported is significant.

Under the "some things never change" banner, I had gone to speak with one of the administrators at the small college where I teach, and was standing near her office, when two gentlemen came through looking for another of our faculty. They had been directed to the reception area where the faculty secretaries are located, having been told one of the secretaries could help them from there. They came right over to me, despite the fact one of the secretaries was at his desk. I saw them look at him, dismiss the possibility that he could be a secretary, and walked right over to me. There really is no way to mistake the fact that this is the secretary's desk. Besides, I found out later from the staff member who had sent them down there, her directions had been very clear. It was also very clear what had hap-

pened: The two gentlemen simply did not think for a moment the guy sitting at the desk was a secretary. I was the only female visible, therefore, I must be the secretary.

Maybe I should have been irked by this, but I was more befuddled than anything else. I'm a full professor, with a significant body of work in the "real" world in addition to my curriculum vitae as a college instructor. I thought attitudes had been given a reworking of late, that these types of assumptions didn't happen. Well, they do. I guess we have more work to do than we thought.

—Molly B.

What feeds this lack of reporting, this reluctance to label an act of sexual harassment just what it is? Labels are powerful. A label of sexual harassment is one of the most powerful labels one can apply. Breaking out of an old tradition, one in which certain behaviors were tolerated with a wink and a nod, and breaking into a new one, where the rules don't seem quite as clear to some of the participants, is not an easy switch.

TRY THIS

For adults: Recognition is important in the workplace. How is accomplishment recognized where you work? Are there tangible symbols of achievement showing in your work space? Are there co-workers in need of some recognition? If you can provide acknowledgment of something noteworthy, whether official or unofficial, do it! A moment in the spotlight is a big morale booster.

For children: Have students bring symbols of accomplishments to class. Suggest they limit the number to three. Discuss what those symbols might be—mention ribbons, trophies, plaques, or any other outward sign that notes a success. Why are these things important, and why do we keep them? Because they remind us we can do things well and we have something to contribute.

For older students: Select one of the contributions from the class, or something you've brought from your own life, either personal, or as a teacher. Use it as an inspiration piece for a flash fiction writing assignment. Set a time limit for the writing and share the results in class.

It must be said sexual harassment does not apply exclusively to women. Current statistics show approximately 11 percent of the sexual harassment claims filed with the Equal Employment Opportunity Commission (EEOC) are by men. It's incumbent on all employers to take all claims of sexual harassment seriously. The number of studies on this experience is not the same as it is for harassment perpetrated against women, but there is no doubt labeling against any man who reported such behavior would be horrendous. The workplace must be made safe for all workers. Labels must not be attached to those who would defend their rights. The label *whistle-blower* is applied to workers who go public with wrongs committed by their companies. If we are to eradicate sexual harassment in the workplace we must assure all they will be safe from similar stigma.

TRY THIS

For older learners: Do some role-playing on the issue of sexual harassment in the workplace. Use scenarios from your own experience, create some based on experiences of others or create something new. Try to incorporate as many of the labels involved in the experiences as you can. What reactions are generated, by the participants and the observers? Does role playing enable you to express the experience more freely?

You can't get there by bus, only by hard work and risk and by not quite knowing what you're doing. What you'll discover will be wonderful. What you'll discover will be yourself.

—Alan Alda

It's possible the reluctance of victims to label or report incidents of sexual harassment may be due, in part, to the fear of negative evaluations from others. We need good empirical studies that systematically examine whether harassment victims who label or report harassment are actually the targets of negative evaluations. Victims may or may not be willing to discuss the topic with trusted colleagues, but in the present climate of documentation for everything, verifiable research is needed.

Even in rape literature, however, victims often do not press charges in order to avoid testifying in court. They often feel their moral character is as much on trial as the accused because, in the past, labeling of the victim has been rife. Similarly, women who report sexual harassment may also feel vulnerable to public scrutiny. They may fear this scrutiny will evoke negative evaluations from others. It was also found women expected to receive severe negative consequences if they reported the incident to some authority, and therefore usually chose not to do so.

I worked in the customer service department of a cable television company. An opening came up for someone to be in charge of an in-house newspaper, so I applied, even though I didn't have a journalism degree. I did have a degree, just not in journalism, although I did have a minor in English and extensive writing experience.

The man they hired was a low-level manger in the company. He didn't have a journalism degree, but he did have an inside track for the job anyway. These days, I wouldn't sit still for something like that. I'd be down at the Human Resource department complaining, but then I took just about everything that came my way. I was mad, and ultimately, when I did quit some months later, I did let them know this was just one incident that formed a pattern in the company. They consistently ignored talent, and they promoted people who didn't deserve it. I wasn't the only one who noticed these things, though. Over a period of time they changed a lot of people at that company.

Did my experience count as sexual harassment? No, not overtly. But it sure wasn't fair, either. And it wasn't smart. I let everybody know what kind of place it was. Everybody except people I should have told, like the EEOC.

—Jeanie S.

As women continue in the workplace, naturally they develop expectations they will advance within their organizations. However, what has happened is the overall advance of women into executive and managerial slots has not happened as it has with men. Instead they have encountered the "glass ceiling." This invisible, but nonetheless real, barrier was preventing them from realizing their professional goals.

Hi, Society!

I was teaching a poetry unit to my fourth graders and had one of those lovely discovery moments: One of my students, a boy who never displayed much interest in language arts, was a gifted natural poet. It was a tricky thing to manage, however, as he seemed anxious that his classmates not be made aware of this. At the beginning of our study, I would collect student work and read it aloud to the class. I gave my kids the option of not having their names read with their work if their piece was chosen that day. Maybe one or two other kids did this, but this boy was fanatic in making sure I didn't say his name. As I read his work often, because it was so good, I was well aware of the panic in his eyes when I'd start to read one of his poems.

I didn't understand his reaction at all, at first. He was fairly popular with his classmates, got along well with most everybody. He had nothing to fear from his work being made public. It was a few weeks down the road that I discovered the source of his concern. We had an open house, and our poetry projects were one of many things we'd been working on that were displayed throughout the classroom. My student's poetry was not on display, at his request. When his father came in that night, he made several pointed remarks about the "sissy" poetry and how happy he'd be when that particular unit was finished. My student was clearly devoted to his father, and just as clearly unhappy about his father's remarks, but he joined in with them. I was both saddened and angered by the whole incident, but there was nothing I could do about it except to tell his father how hard the class had worked, and how important it had been to explore this type of literature.

I think what saddened me the most was my student had been so taken with poetry he had been doing extra credit work all on his own, just because he loved it. After this evening, that stopped. The next thing to appear in his journal, and indeed the theme that ran through it for the remainder of the year were his recounting of weekends spent riding in off-road vehicles out in the desert. To each his own, but I missed the poetic insights of a boy who had shown real promise.

—Fran R.

As with other labels, a kernel of truth has given rise to workplace stereotypes and labeling. There is some evidence to suggest job groupings by gender, such as clerical (typically female) and physical (typically male), may not be sexist. Some evidence indicates natural gender-based right-brain/left-brain tendencies have contributed in large part to the common distribution of tasks in any organization. We should, however, still encourage talent and interest wherever we find it. It's also true we would be well served to start letting our children in on these clues when they are at an age to understand these differences. In every group there are those who are more comfortable going against what is typical. How often has a girl with natural mechanical tendencies been denied the opportunity to explore that part of her skill set? How often has a boy with natural tendencies toward occupations like nursing or the arts been turned away or denied the chance because there was an assumption the boy was gay?

TRY THIS

What are "boy jobs" and "girl jobs"? Younger students may have some revealing ideas on this topic. This can be a class discussion or for very young students it can be a subject they can dictate a story about. Older students, particularly those in middle or high school, will have definite ideas about workplace issues and what kinds of jobs they are interested in pursuing.

For further discussion: How have ideas about particular jobs changed in student's families? Is there anyone in their family who has had, or currently has, a job more often followed by the opposite gender?

If women are expected to do the same work as men, we must teach them the same things.

—Aristotle

Think attitudes have changed? Not as much as they should have. I have a male friend who's a registered nurse. He happens to be 6 feet 4 inches and about 225 pounds—a big guy. He's also the last guy people look at when they want to talk to "the nurse." He'll have people come up to him thinking he's the orderly, the janitor or even the doctor, but never the nurse. He said it used to bug him, but now he just laughs at it.

—Erin H.

Changing roles apply to men as well. In particular, the number of men adopting the role of primary caretaker for young children has increased dramatically. They face challenges from those who continue to hold the outdated ideas only women should be the primary caretakers of young children. They often have to deal with questions like, "What did you do in the real world?" Of course the most significant label for men in this situation is "Mr. Mom." Cultural conditioning aside, there is a growing swell of respect for men who make the choice to raise their children. There are even some studies that suggest children of relationships where the mother is the primary breadwinner and the father the primary caretaker benefit because the mother is even more involved with the children during her nonwork hours. Networking, one of the mainstays of the business world, has moved into the world of the "stay-at-home-dad" by way of magazines and ever more numbers of websites.

EYE OPENER

What's the worst case of labeling you've encountered in the workplace? Did you have any recourse? Were you able to bring about any change?

Senior Moments

One gerontologist maintains elderly populations suffer from negative stereotyping more than any other identifiable social group. She argues preconceived ideas about the elderly, including their thinking, physical ability, health, sociability, personality, and work capability drive these negative stereotypes. Certainly it's a truism of American culture increasing age seems to represent decreasing value as a human being. According to mass media scholar Joshua Meyrowitz, old people are respected to the extent they can behave like young people—to the extent they remain capable of working, enjoying sex, exercising, and taking care of themselves.

It's also true in Western culture, we do not value our senior citizens as "elders" with wisdom and experience who should be treasured and respected. (Native Americans are an exception, as are some immigrant cultures.) The dominance of media in popular culture, with its emphasis on youth and beauty, undoubtedly influences to a large extent the value, or lack of it, placed on seniors. Certainly there is a dearth of appearances, either on television or in film, of seniors. When they are portrayed in commercials, it's generally a negative stereotype of a cranky senior, or an infirm elderly person unable to get around on his or her own.

Part of the problem may rest in the fact children today often have very little opportunity to interact with older people. Our society tends more and more toward the nuclear rather than the extended family. Young couples often move away from their families to find good jobs elsewhere, leaving behind their parents and grandparents. There is some hope in getting children better acquainted with the older generations. For example, an after-school program had school-age children and seniors working together and a living history project in a southern California high school sends high-school juniors and seniors out to interview their grandparents to obtain their life stories and integrate them into their history curriculum.

TRY THIS

For parents: If your school does not have a living history program, talk to the principal and suggest starting one. Volunteer to help coordinate it and ask for help from teachers and the PTA. Start with your own family. If you have grandparents living near you, talk with them. Find someone from any groups you're a part of, whether a church group, a book club, or someone you meet on your daily walk. If your interest in someone is genuine, chances are they'll be willing to participate.

For teachers: Get involved with a living history project. Older children will be able to handle a field trip to a convalescent home if they are properly prepared for it. You might institute your own Grandparent's Day, independent of the Hallmark holiday. Have children bring in photos of their grandparents, write and talk about them, draw pictures of them, or even bring in the genuine article! Explore cultural diversity in your classroom by learning the word for *grandparent* in other languages. Make a banner using these names.

Don't ever think "they're going to be around—I can ask about that some other day," because that "some other day" can quickly turn into "never." When you're a kid, you don't always appreciate the stories your parents tell you about when they were kids, especially if they're stories you've heard many times. That's the way it was with me. I didn't really start to get a sense of how important those stories were until I had kids myself. Maybe it was something about connecting the generations that hit me once I became a mother.

I started listening a lot more closely, and then my mother passed away, and I thought of how I had decided to get a tape recorder and get her to tell stories of her growing up in Britain during World War II. I didn't act fast enough when the idea hit me, and then she was gone. My father had lots of colorful tales of his days in the Merchant Marine, and again, I didn't get them down on tape and now they're mostly gone except for little fragments of memories. It's a shame. I wish I had done more when I had the chance.

—Monica R.

The old believe everything,
the middle-aged suspect everything,
the young know everything.

—Oscar Wilde

It's hell getting old, and I don't mean my health, or aches and pains, or living on a fixed income, or any of that stuff. I'll tell you why. People talk about you like you weren't even in the room, or if they do pretend to notice you're there, they talk to you like you were about five years old. It's insulting. With all I've lived through, I deserve a little more courtesy than that, I can tell you. I don't like to be called "dear'"and I don't like people discussing me like I had disappeared. I'm pretty lucky. My health is still very good, so I don't need any more help than anybody else, but the people at the doctor's office take my elbow like I'm gonna fall down. I'm not, and if I were, I'd ask for help. Oh, and another thing. Why do people insist on making jokes about my love life? I'll tell you why. They think it's cute to make jokes about senior citizens even having a love life. My husband's been gone for a long time. At my age, it's hard to find somebody. By the way, it's hard at your age, too, isn't it? I don't make cutesy jokes about your love life. We'd have to be a lot closer friends to do that, but anybody who thinks because I'm over fifty I'm fair game, I'm not.

—Dorothy J.,
legally a senior citizen

One day I'm a fully capable pilot, flying 737 jets full of passengers. The next day I can't do that. What happened? I had a birthday. I turned sixty and now the rules say I can't fly.

—airline captain on being
forced to retire upon his
sixtieth birthday

―――――――――――――――――

Middle age is when you meet so many people that every new person you meet reminds you of someone else.

—Ogden Nash

―――――――――――――――――

From the ridiculous attitudes about our elders, we go to the sublime:

We have a wonderful, positive program at our school that puts kids and seniors together in an after-school program. It runs daily over the course of a semester. They have kids from third through fifth grade involved with seniors from our community who want to be involved with the school. Lots of these kids have a tough time at home. Many of them are latchkey kids and their parents are gone quite a bit. The seniors are terrific role models. They do arts and crafts, help with homework and work one on one with the kids. There's nothing like that amount of direct attention to help a kid who's struggling.

My son loved it. He was doing fine with his schoolwork, but I'm a single parent, and though I was giving him lots of attention, his dad was hard on him, and it was hurting. The seniors always enjoyed his enthusiasm and bouncy spirit; he had the time of his life. It was definitely a win-win thing. My parents were both dead and my son's other grandparents lived too far away for regular contact. It's great, too, that the lesson about older people still contributing to their communities can be taught so subtly but effectively. I'll always be grateful for that program. He had to really toe the line to get selected, as there were a limited number of spots, and it was a privilege that could be taken away if there were any problems in his regular class. My son worked hard to stay in the program. It did his self esteem a world of good.

—Jenn E.

Remember the trouble we experienced when we were very young, just starting out, and were judged for our lack of experience? So, too, are the elderly judged. Age discrimination against the elderly is an important issue. It's a subtle thing. It's there, but it's like a ghost. You can believe in it, because you've experienced it. You can believe in it because others you trust have experienced it. Getting proof and getting independent verification may be another thing entirely.

Old age is not so bad when you consider the alternatives.
—Maurice Chevalier

I worked in chemistry for years, until I got laid off. There I was, with thirty years of experience, but I'm in my mid-fifties. It took a long time, but I found another job. That went fine until that company went belly-up, and there I was again, looking for work. Well now I'm in my early sixties and nobody wants to hire me. They can't tell you that, and they sure won't, but don't be fooled for an instant. Even companies with huge turnover, where they'd be happy if somebody stayed for six months, they won't hire me, and I'm likely to stay four to six years. I've got all the experience, I'm willing to work for what they're paying—and it's not much. Don't let anybody tell you anything different. There's rampant age discrimination out there. I'm retired now. I don't want to be, but I am.
—Steve R.

I've done secretarial work almost since I left high school, so I'm really experienced. I had a good position with a good company, but they merged with another company, so lots of people lost their jobs. They always tell you that won't happen. Anyway, I couldn't get anything right away so I signed up with a temp agency, which was okay for a while, but at my age, I want a steady income and a steady job. So I do this for nearly a year and at last, a temp job works into a permanent one. Things go along until once again, our lab merges with another. This time I keep my job, but I get a new boss. It just isn't working, so I leave. I go on the job hunt again, but now I'm sixty. I've got all kinds of great references. Everybody I worked for has always been pleased with my work, but they want twenty-some-things they can pay less, not somebody with my experience. At one place where I applied, there were two women in their twenties filling out their applications and I hear them whispering behind my back, "Did you see how old she was?" It hurt.

You can tell when they're expecting somebody younger. Some hide it better than others, but you can always tell. Of course they're not going to say anything about your age because you can sue them. They don't have to, there are always other reasons for not hiring you. I got hired by the university to do temp work there, so I work in one department or another. Some of the jobs are really awful, but most are all right. But I'll never make the kind of money again that I could, with my skills. It stinks getting older. Why do people who do the hiring have that attitude? It's like everything I've learned over the years has no value. I hear people say because we're older, we won't stay as long, that we'll retire and quit. There are two things wrong with that. The first is turnover in some of these jobs is high anyway. Older workers, on the other hand, are usually so grateful just to get the job that we stay. The second thing is most of us have to work longer before we can retire anyway.

—Mary O.

TRY THIS

For teachers: Have a discussion about age labels. Have students project what they will be like at ages sixty, seventy, and eighty. How would they like others to treat them when they are old? Are there significant seniors in their lives? Do they feel the seniors in their lives are treated the way they hope to be? Will their own treatment of the elderly change now?

True or false quiz:
- Growing old means living in a nursing home.
  False. Fewer than five percent of our elderly live in such facilities. Most can live in their own homes and take care of themselves.
- Mental capacity fades as we get older.
  False. Although it's true our style of learning tends to change as we get older, healthy seniors are just as capable of learning as anyone else. In fact, since older learners do best when they're focused on a topic, this time of life is well suited to learning things for which there may not have been time earlier.
- Seniors should avoid physical activity.
  False. As long as someone is healthy, they have every reason to exercise. Mental stimulation and emotional connections are also important.

The "age is a state of mind" concept is perhaps nowhere better illustrated than in the case of Dr. Jack Ward. In November, 1999, Ward, then seventy-five years old, was awarded his Ph.D. from Hallam University in England. His accomplishment was remarkable for more than the age at which he achieved it. Jack Ward was branded a dunce when he was a young student. He dropped out of school.

Like many others of his era, but to a lesser extent today, Dr. Ward suffers from dyslexia. His condition went unrecognized. It was his wife, Audrey, who taught him to read and write. He then attended night school. After retiring from his government job, the grandfather of five returned to his studies, continuing even after he suffered a stroke.

TRY THIS

See how many students are familiar with the word *dunce*. Have them discuss how they think Dr. Ward might have felt earning his doctorate at the age of seventy-five. What do they think Dr. Ward might have wanted to say to the people who labeled him when he was a child, if he'd had the chance? Discuss the origins of the word dunce and make comparisons with more contemporary terms having the same meaning.

Our culture is so youth obsessed, we're ready to accept any number of myths about aging. Here are just a few:
- Old Age Myth #1 To be old is to be sick.

- Old Age Myth #2 You can't teach an old dog new tricks.
- Old Age Myth #3 The horse is out of the barn.
- Old Age Myth #4 The secret to successful aging is to choose your parents wisely.
- Old Age Myth #5 The lights may be on, but the voltage is low.
- Old Age Myth #6 The elderly don't pull their own weight.

TRY THIS

For teachers: How old is old? Why? Poll the class and graph the results. What are some things you shouldn't do if you're old? Are there limits as to what we should allow elderly people to do? What does old look like?

To me, old age is always fifteen years older than I am.
—Bernard Baruch

As a society we're obsessed with the negative rather than the positive aspects of aging. Truth lies in accepting that scientific evidence clearly points away from these stereotypes. America must quickly get a grip on the new reality in view of the hoards of over-sixty baby boomers to shortly descend upon it.

Older people are much more likely to age well than to become decrepit and dependent. Studies conclude older Americans are generally healthy. Even in advanced old age, an overwhelming majority of the population has little functional disability and, with time, the portion that is disabled is being reduced. Much of this is because of huge reductions in acute infectious illnesses in the twentieth century and more recent declines in precursors to chronic disease such as high blood pressure, high cholesterol levels, and smoking.

Research shows older people can, and do, learn new things. Three key factors predict strong mental function in old age: (1) regular physical activity; (2) a strong social support system; and (3) belief in one's ability to handle what life has to offer. More and more we are learning that stimulating the mind, being active learners throughout our lives, is beneficial for the young and the old. There is evidence to suggest, as well, continuous learning may be one avenue of fighting the onset of Alzheimer's disease.

I was in Florida recently working one of the big hotels. The crowd was mostly Senior Citizens. I was a smash. It was the first time I ever got a "crouching ovation."

—Phyllis Diller

TRY THIS

Ask students why they should care about the elderly. Fish for answers like "because I'll be old one day, too," or "because seniors are a valuable part of our community."

Although Western physicians are slowly altering their attitudes about illness to encompass the mind/body connection, in general they are quick to dismiss a holistic approach to healing. It's much faster and easier, once a diagnosis is made, to announce it and treat the problem rather than take the patient's life and feelings into account. *Alternative* can be a nasty label in the parlance of some doctors. It can carry meanings ranging from mildly kooky to downright dangerous.

Physicians are powerful. If a doctor tells a patient they are dying, some will accept the sentence without challenge. Others might seek alternative treatment but, without the backing of a trusted practitioner, success is less likely. Patients can't "cheat death." However, in some circumstances, it may be possible to hold it off for much longer than a traditional Western medicine program might allow.

My father was diagnosed with emphysema, and his last hospitalization was serious. We had to fight to get him sent home rather than to a nursing home, but even so, I was very upset with the doctor. He made it clear my dad wasn't going to live another six months. Well, there's no doubt my father was in bad shape, but what the doctor failed to realize was the hospital was making him sicker. He felt miserable there, completely unable to rally his emotional strength and determination, his stubbornness. He'd never been one to talk about his feelings, either, so he couldn't articulate that.

He knew his time was going to be limited, but he knew, too, he'd just feel better living with my brother in his home. The problem was he was feeling so bad physically he couldn't really advocate for himself. Anyway, this doctor should not have said what he said, at least the way he said it. Once we made it clear, not only did my father have a place to live, he had more than enough support to help him, he agreed to release my father despite the staggering home healthcare he would need, at least initially. I just wish he could have been more supportive in his attitude out loud.

My dad was stubborn. Once he was in an environment where he felt better about being there, he made a remarkable comeback. He was still suffering from his lung disease, but he recovered enough strength and health to live nearly two years after his discharge, and it was a good quality of life. Yes, he had his limitations, but he was well able to tolerate them. We could take him places. We could take him to the doctor's visits he needed. He was able to live a reasonably normal life. The doctor was amazed at how well he was doing, what a difference he could see. I hope my father's story helped change something in this doctor's approach to other patients in similar circumstances. You have to always take people's lives into account when you're talking about their deaths. The doctor wasn't deliberately trying to sabotage anything. He was just clinical when he could have been kind. I don't know. Maybe like other doctors he's forced into a quick, clinical approach because he's just not allowed the luxury of time. I hope not.

—Elsie J.

A recent review of a book by a physician who promotes encompassing a variety of techniques suggested patients seek more from their physicians than mere diagnoses—that patients are asking for more emotional and psychic connection with their healers. The doctor who wrote the review (written by a fellow physician) felt his first- and second-year students shared this ideal and this book may well be a way of returning to it. For some doctors, the word *holistic* is a label synonymous with *flake* and, as such, is quickly dismissed. Holistic healing treats each person holistically—they treat the person as a whole and not simply as a collection of symptoms. A recent article appearing in the *Journal of the American Medical Association* was eloquent in its description of the healing power of the handwritten word. Part of the power associated with that healing is the caring and the time associated with the act of writing.

The good physician treats the disease but the great physician treats the patient.

—Sir William Osler

TRY THIS

For teachers: Ask students to create a magical formula to heal disease. Discuss healing, what it means to be ill, and what makes them feel better when they're sick. Discuss what sick looks like. What do their families do when someone is ill? What are some of the things that make them more comfortable during minor illnesses? Do they have certain comfort foods? Do they watch a favorite movie or read a particular book? Share some of your comfort mechanisms.

Did you have any thoughts that when you left school you wouldn't have to deal with name-calling and labeling any more? Has it really turned out that way? Onward, to some positive ways of dealing with the world.

Chapter Seven

The Label's Off—
Now What?

One can never consent to creep when one feels an impulse to soar.
—Helen Keller

A tart temper never mellows with age, and a sharp tongue is
the only edged tool that grows keener with constant use.
—Washington Irving

A king said to a hermit, "Come with me and I'll give you power."
"I have all the power I know how to use," answered the hermit.
"Come," said the king, "I will give you wealth."
"I have no wants money can supply," said the hermit.
"I will give you honor," said the king.
"Honor cannot be given, it must be earned," the hermit said.
"If you come," said the king, trying one last time, "I will give
you happiness."
How, he thought, could anyone turn down such an offer?
"No," said the man of solitude, "there is no happiness without
liberty, and he who follows cannot be free."
"You shall have liberty too," said the king.
"Then I will stay where I am," said the old man.
And all the king's courtiers thought the hermit a fool.

EYE OPENER

Do you think the hermit was a fool? Did the king think the hermit was a fool? What was the king offering, and why was he trying so hard to get the hermit to return with him?

By now we've talked about labels, stereotyping, and bullying, and other behaviors that don't do much but set the world back a few paces. We're all aware of what needs to be done. *Now what?* Too often we hear we can't change the world, and it's true. It was true at the beginning of this book, and it's true now. However, just like at the beginning of the book, you *can* still change your little corner of the world. Take everything you don't like about labels, and do what you can to change.

If you don't say something that comes to your mind, if you hold your temper when it's most difficult for you to do so, you've changed the world. You had the opportunity to hurt somebody but held your tongue. You achieved a victory. If you could have called somebody a name, labeled him or her in some fashion, even if you were *right*, and you took the high road instead, you changed the world. It isn't easy, but it is simple.

Too often the temptation is to just throw up our hands because a problem seems too big to handle. Even trying to get help can seem like an insurmountable task (though it isn't). Ever feel like giving up? Think you've got no friends, no place to go, and no hope? People calling you names to the point you'd like to give up? One man might have felt the same way early in his life. At one time you couldn't pick up a newspaper without finding this man's work inside, or go to a store without finding his work on cards, T-shirts, and just about anything else you could imagine. He was considered a failure when he was growing up. His contemporaries thought him a washout. He had few friends and no dates and didn't even pass all his classes.

When he felt especially bad, he'd do some drawings to cheer himself up. He even got enough gumption to send some to Walt Disney, but they were rejected. He didn't give up. He kept drawing and drew a cartoon about a boy just like him. The cartoon—*Peanuts*. The man was Charles Schultz.

EYE OPENER

What has been the biggest effect of labeling in your life? Have you seen a change in attitude, overall, with regard to labeling?

TRY THIS

For everyone in the group: Buy several packages of labels and write as many labels you can recall having been used on you—anything you didn't like, that hurt, wasn't fair or accurate—anything you'd like gone. Stick them on your clothing. As a group, call out "Labels off!" Then, on the count of three everybody tears off their labels and rips them up, throwing the pieces in the air.

Treat people as individuals. Accept and respect their differences.

TO THINK ABOUT

Children try. Adults do.

She grew up as one of seventeen children in a poor black family. Segregation was the norm. At four, her left leg was crippled by polio and she was told by doctors she would need a leg brace for the rest of her life. She didn't like the idea and refused to believe it, so at age twelve she took off the brace and never used it again.

She was tired of sitting and watching everybody else get in the game. She decided she would get right in there with them. Before long, she was the star of her high school basketball team. Ed Temple, coach of the Tennessee State track team, noticed how fast and agile she was. He invited her to train with the team. Again she did well, becoming the fastest sprinter on the team. She made the 1960 Olympic track team, winning three gold medals and many hearts with her determination.

Who was she? She was Wilma Rudolph, a young woman who refused to be conquered by her physical problems. She overcame polio to be known as "the fastest woman in the world."

To be nobody but yourself in a world which is doing its best night and day to make you like everybody else means to fight the hardest battle any human being can fight and never stop fighting.
—e. e. cummings

The Label's Off—Now What?

Erase the words can't *and* but *from your vocabulary.*

Affirmation and inspiration are the focus of this chapter. Affirmations are intended to change or reinforce attitudes. By definition, they're positive. Putting negative terms into a proposition defeats the purpose. As you learn to make affirmations, write them down so you will remember exactly what you want to say. Keep them short and very specific. Personalize them with your name.

You can't go wrong with the good old golden rule. If you don't like something said or done to you, don't say or do it to others. Even if somebody does or says something to you, nothing is accomplished by your returning fire.

Benjamin Franklin once set out to write a book extolling specific techniques for perfecting oneself through the development of virtues. It was to be called *The Art of Virtue*, but he never finished it. Franklin also intended to create an organization and secret society based on that idea. Because Franklin's idea was to make the society universal and nonsectarian, secrecy was important. In those days, you could be charged with heresy. He believed strongly if even a few people committed their lives to developing the virtues of being a good person, and secretly recruited friends and family, over time it would spread from one person to the next. Eventually they would have created a new and better society. The threat of heresy charges is now gone from most societies, and we can openly pursue such a wonderful nondenominational program to treat each other with dignity and respect—without the use of labels or stereotypes.

You must give some time to your fellow men. Even if it's a little thing, do something for others—something for which you get no pay but the privilege of doing it.

—Albert Schweitzer

Patty C. tells about how we can overcome the negatives in life:

I spent way too many years of my life being a victim. I really was a victim of abuse, but I took much longer than I would have wished, now, to deal with it and find a new way to live. Being a victim is a skill that, once you get good at it, you really hate to give it up. You get to let yourself off the hook for lots of stuff in your life, even if it's true stuff. You get to wallow in what somebody else did to you and it's never your responsibility if you don't get what you want or need. There's usually a pretty good measure of sympathy that goes along with it, too.

That's not to put down people who were, and are, in worse shape than me. For some, there just isn't a way out. I don't want to sound cold, because that's not the way I am. I'm saying for me, it was possible to get up and get out. The past is part of my memory. I'll forgive, but not forget,

If I were truly a good person, maybe I'd do both, but right now, I want to remember enough that I don't let the same things happen to me again. I can move on, having learned what I've learned. It is possible to let the past teach and not restrain.

The past is in the past. Grow from it and put it behind you.

In me the need to talk is a primary impulse, and I can't help saying right off what comes to my tongue.

—Miguel de Cervantes

Few stories are as inspirational to us as that of Helen Keller, and of her teacher and companion, Annie Sullivan. Helen was a normal child until age two, when a virus left her deaf and blind. At that point, little could be done for her until the wonderful Annie came into her life. It was the miracle of Annie's patience and love that brought Helen Keller back from the wild darkness of her existence into the light of the world that would benefit from her intelligence and compassion. This story is proof we can overcome our present limitations.

Use affirmations to transform negative thinking. They are simple, but I didn't say they were easy. Like any new habit you want to culti-vate, it will require practice to make affirmations part of your life and make them work for you. This will be harder if you're more negatively natured. It's easier to start out with a positive than to change a negative. Rather than saying, "I will stop being a couch potato," say, "I will walk thirty minutes every Monday, Wednesday, and Friday." The more specific the goal, the greater likelihood for success. Self-knowledge is important in setting goals and affirmations. If you hate walking, you'll probably quit very soon (if you get started at all). However, if you love bicycle riding, use that knowledge to empower your affirmation. And yes, it helps to have a sense of humor, too!

As we started this book, the point was made that one goal was to achieve awareness. This awareness will help with affirmations. In order for them to take effect, to help you make changes in your life, you'll need to be aware of what you want to accomplish, improve or eliminate from your life.

One effective technique is visualization. Picture in your mind what you want to do. You can do this just about anywhere or any time. Some use it to send away an image they don't like. I think it's more powerful to picture something you *do* want. Again, knowing yourself will determine what works best for you.

When I was pregnant with my first child, we attended childbirth classes. We learned breathing techniques and lots of other ideas for making the birth of our babies the best experience it could be, and to minimize the pain as much as possible. We were asked at one class to picture a focal point, something we could concentrate on during contractions. It could be anything we wanted, something in the room, or something we would bring from home and that would go with us into the birthing suite once the time came.

Of course I forgot to bring something with me to that class, so I had to find something in the room. To this day I still use the two focal points I found that night. (I can never do anything the easy way!) The first was the brass eagle atop the flag pole for our state flag flying in the auditorium where our class was held. The other was a memory of something I had seen on a vacation, because the instructor also said we could use a memory. To this day (and my child is now almost fifteen), when I'm stressed I can count on those focal points. The instructor told me she'd never seen anybody concentrate as hard as I did that night.

It's served me well. I've used them when I've been ill to get through the worst of the pain. I've used them when I'm driving and the full moon seems to be affecting the way people drive and I'm afraid I might not make it home. I've used it to screen out thoughts that I'll never finish a project, and I've used it to control my anger on occasion. But it works. It really, really works.

—Tracy K.

Great spirits have always encountered violent opposition from mediocre minds.

—Albert Einstein

One of the greatest minds of all time was Albert Einstein. His early life was marked not by spectacular success, but rather by failure and mediocrity. He didn't do well in school and went to work in a patent office. It was there that he developed his phenomenal theory of relativity. Despite his genius, he remained a humble man. Who are you to do any less?

Never be bullied into silence.
Never allow yourself to be made a victim.

Accept no one's definition of your life, but define yourself.

—Harvey Fierstien

TRY THIS

For older learners: What is one thing about yourself you'd like to improve? Set a goal for accomplishing it and list three ways you can do it.

For younger learners: Their goals may not be as much about self-improvement as learning skills like tying their shoes or riding a bike. It can also be about behaviors like taking turns, not poking their neighbors in line or other practical skills. Be sure to include rewards for success.

For our summer session before we started high school in the fall, we had to try a whole lot of exercises about trust, and stuff like that, and it made me nervous, but I did it, because we had to, and if everybody in our group didn't do it, then we'd lose out on other things we wanted to do. Believe me, you do not want to be the one who makes that happen! After those activities were over, I understood better why the teacher made us do them, and I appreciated them. I still didn't like them, but that's partly because new things make me nervous. Then at the end of the session, we had to pick one thing about ourselves to set as a goal for the coming year.

I thought it would be hard to pick one thing, but when the time came, it wasn't hard at all. I picked "I will think more positively." My mom is always telling me that, because sometimes I'll get a big project or assignment or something, and I'll get panicky and say, "I can't do it." And she'll always say, "Well, if you tell yourself that, of course you can't." That's why I thought of it. We wrote those things on pieces of board and then we got to decorate the board and try to break it. It was cool. I broke my board, too!

—Jessica E., ninth-grader

Make affirmations part of your daily life.

I wanted to be a writer, but I had young children and my husband was not supportive. I didn't really believe in affirmations, either, which is the funny thing, because I started doing it out of sheer desperation. I think it was a book on writing that hooked me on it. It wasn't that part that got me hooked, at first, it was a very simple little writing exercise that made me think, Yeah, I can do this. I really can! So I treated myself to the book, took it home, and sat down to try that little exercise.

It worked. I did one, and then the next day I squeezed out a few minutes and did another, took the book into the bathroom if I had to, and found time to read it more and more. I came to the exercise that said if you wanted to be a writer you had to wake up each morning and tell yourself that. What helped even more, at the time, was reading the part that even if you didn't quite believe it in your heart and soul, it was important to keep saying it, to keep writing, even if it was only a little. Eventually, that writer said, eventually, you will believe it. You'll have taught yourself that truth and it will be a real truth. I haven't made the best-seller lists yet, but I'm still writing, and getting

better all the time. I encourage my kids, too, and they're all accom-
plished writers.

—Val B.

Our relationships are central to our lives. Complacency or neglect can damage them. Like most living things, they need attention. Here are some affirmations to help. These are merely samples. Use your unique knowledge of yourself and your situation to create others specific to your life.

- I must build a loving relationship with myself before I can share my gift with others.
- The gift I give myself is the belief I can follow my journey and trust my inner self.
- I am a work in progress: good today, even better tomorrow.
- I can be honest and direct in communicating my needs to others.
- Today I will respect and love myself by recognizing my own needs first.

Small steps will still complete the journey.

When you are fascinated with the world, the world is fascinated with you.

—Stephanie Smith

Another way to look at an affirmation is to think of it as an exercise in building up. Self-esteem is implied. Students and teachers can help build self-esteem in each other by:

- Smiles
- Being accepting and supportive
- Communicating and cooperating with each other
- Encouraging each other
- Giving and accepting responsibility
- Listening
- Not using put-downs
- Praising good work and good effort
- Respecting others

The Label's Off—Now What?

Keeping in mind Gardener's learning styles, find a way to represent an affirmation that reflects your style. You could make bookmarks of your favorite quotations or use your own words. Make some for yourself and more for gifts. A great way to get that affirmation working is to pass it around. Do a painting. You can inscribe it with an affirmation, or just let yourself react with color to how the thoughts make you feel. Take a photo and mount it. Buy or make candles. Specific scents will arouse emotions. Learn flower arranging. Flowers brighten spaces for everyone. They create a zone in which passers by might have a lighter moment. They'll stop to admire the flowers or enjoy their scent.

I started buying flowers for my desk at work because I wasn't too thrilled with my job and I found having the flowers there really put me in a better mood, boosted my attitude. I found I had a talent for arranging, and it gave me a wonderful artistic outlet where there weren't very many in the job I was doing. Something else happened, too, that I hadn't anticipated when I started out doing this. Because I had an eye for color and arranging, my flowers caught the attention of most of the people passing by my desk. I sat in a high traffic spot in my workplace and all day long people would pass by. So many people stopped to say something about the flowers. Sometimes it was only to say, "Hey, those are really pretty." Others stopped to talk about them, to admire them, ask me where I'd bought them, and often we'd have nice conversations. I liked all of it, but especially, I think, the ones who just said a few words, because I knew they were the ones who probably wouldn't have said anything at all. The flowers were a terrific ice-breaker.

—Sue L.

Do something new! You don't have to dog sled across a glacier to do something new and brave. Give yourself permission to do a new *small* thing. Some people are explorers, some people are not. Doing even a little thing can help us to gain confidence. If you are alone, go to a movie or out to dinner—alone. It's surprising how many single people still feel stigmatized by being alone in public places. If you can find a different route to go home, do that once a week. You might see something you've never seen before. You might see somebody doing something extraordinary. You might encounter a plant you've never seen before.

TRY THIS

Look outside your culture for an opportunity. It can be hard to step outside our comfort zones, but it can be rewarding and educational. Learn something new... try food from another culture, learn about another culture's ceremony or ritual. In most larger cities the population is very likely compiled of dozens of cultural groups. Open a newspaper, ask at the library or pick up any one of the free papers available just about anywhere—you're bound to find something.

I will forever be grateful to the wonderful, understanding, and giving soul who was my child's sixth grade teacher. She understood him where many didn't. She appreciated his quick mind and humor. She realized a sensitive soul when she saw one. She helped ground him by letting him know she thought he was pretty neat. She helped him see when he'd made a mistake without scarring him in the process. She did this for every child that came her way, but it meant the most to me because this was my kid. She followed up at the end of the year, too, and made sure he got hooked up with other teachers for seventh grade, ones who would follow up. As far as I'm concerned, she deserves a medal.

—Tasha Y.

TRY THIS

Is there a convalescent center in your neighborhood? Volunteer to help out. Most are habitually understaffed and often have residents who have only infrequent visitors, if any. Don't think you have enough time? Nobody does. Maybe all you can do is one morning a month. Do what you can. Every little bit helps somebody.

I really like working at nursing homes. You can hear some great stories from the people there!

—Tenth grader, on volunteer opportunities
with her high school service club

I wanted to help at my kids' schools, but I was working two jobs, so my time was limited. Still, I stopped by the library on back-to-school night and talked with the librarian to broach the subject. I told her I wanted to help out but I could only give her about an hour once a week. She was delighted! They had so much to do they were grateful for any help at all, but it wasn't only that. She was just pleased by any parent offering to help—really buying into the "every bit counts" thing in a big way. When I showed up for the first morning, I was made very welcome. Never underestimate the power of one hour. The work I did that day made it possible for a lot of new books to go out on the shelves. Not bad for a small investment.

—Brad J.

TRY THIS

Meals on Wheels, a food delivery organization for the elderly, is another opportunity to give back to your community. Even a limited time commitment won't stop you from participating. Look them up in the white pages of your phone book and give them a call.

I used to deliver for Meals on Wheels. When my kids were little and if I couldn't find a babysitter, I'd put them in their car seats and take them with me, because this was important for my mental health. It took me outside myself even if my children were with me. I loved doing my route, even if it was only twice a month. It didn't take long before I got to know my seniors and I looked forward to seeing them. Maybe it's selfish: I got as much out of doing that as anybody got from me bringing the meals. It was one of the best experiences of my life.

—Tanya L.

To sing, to laugh, to dream,
To walk in my own way

—Edmond Rostand

Some guidelines about affirmations:

● Use the *present* or *past tense*. Do not use the future tense. It sounds odd, but you want your mind to know it has already *happened*.

● Use the most *positive* words you can.

- As previously stated, *write them down*. Keep them short and specific.
- *Believe*. Always believe what you are saying is happening. The more you believe, the stronger the affirmation.
- Be *repetitive* and *persistent*. It helps to set them in your head and in your unconscious being.
- Set aside a *specific time* daily for your meditations, affirmations, and visualizations. This will help set a pattern for you so you will do them daily.

Think of affirmations as stickers for your brain. Pick the ones you like and the ones you'll use. A few suggestions for personal affirmations:

- I can see myself successful in a job that challenges me and enriches me personally or professionally.
- I wake up refreshed and eager to tackle what the day will bring.
- I feel invigorated by my exercise program.
- I am relaxed and calm.
- I see myself as a winner.
- I never give up.
- I will make time for myself to be alone and think my thoughts, to renew myself. I deserve this. I need this to maintain my serenity, for myself and those around me.

An idealist is one who, on noticing that a rose smells better than a cabbage, concludes that it will also make better soup.

—H. L. Mencken

Museums and art stores are also sources of pleasure and inspiration. Doubtless it will seem strange to many that the hand unaided by sight can feel action, sentiment, beauty in the cold marble; and yet it is true that I derive genuine pleasure from touching great works of art. As my finger tips trace line and curve, they discover the thought and emotion which the artist has portrayed.

—Helen Keller

The Label's Off—Now What?

Think of all the beauty still left around you and be happy.
—Anne Frank

Create your own oasis. You may be short on space and time but, find some of both to make a little oasis for yourself. It could be something as simple as a bubble bath once a week. It's time for you, time to reflect and refresh. Make it part of your routine, just like your other affirmations.

Try combining the affirmation with a Try This activity. The more active you are in asserting affirmations, the more likely you are to make them true.

Some affirmations for daily living:

- I acknowledge all of my feelings because I am in touch with my feelings.
- I am loving and accepting of others. This is how I create lasting friendships.
- I love and accept myself.
- I am unique.
- I trust my inner being to lead me in the right path.
- My inner vision is always clear and focused.

Students can make these types of affirmations as well. We do it now in most classrooms, we just don't call them affirmations. By telling students to come to class prepared to listen, with their homework completed, we are in essence asking them to make affirmations regarding their work.

Affirmations for health:

- I have the power to control my health.
- I am in control of my health and wellness.
- I have abundant energy, vitality, and well-being.
- I am healthy in all aspects of my being.
- I do not fear being unhealthy because I know I control my own body.
- I am always able to maintain my ideal weight.
- I am filled with energy to do all the daily activities in my life.

- My mind is at peace.
- I love and care for my body and it cares for me.

TRY THIS

For younger learners: Gather pictures from the basic food groups. Have the children classify the pictures, make charts using the pictures or make a booklet about food. Make them Food Deputies and, at their swearing-in ceremony, have them take an oath to try new (especially healthy) foods whenever they can, even if just a bite. All students can make some determinations regarding their health, such as:

- I will watch a half hour less television this week.
- Instead of watching TV when I come home, I will play outside with my friends.
- I will have an apple for a snack instead of potato chips.
- I will drink water instead of a soda.

We can use affirmations to improve any and all aspects of our lives. The following are affirmations for abundance:

- I am a success in all I do.
- Everything I touch returns riches to me.
- I am always productive.
- My work is always recognized positively.
- I respect my abilities and always work to my full potential.
- I am constantly adding to my income.
- I always spend money wisely.
- I always have enough money for all I need.
- I am rewarded for all the work I do.

Affirmations for peace and harmony:

- I am at peace with myself.
- I am always in harmony with the universe.
- I am filled with the love of my Higher Power.
- I am at peace with those around me.
- I have provided a harmonious place for myself and those I love.
- The more honest I am with those around me, the more love is returned to me.

152

- I express anger in appropriate ways so peace and harmony are balanced at all times.
- I am at one with my inner child.

Affirmations for my spirituality:
- I am free to be myself.
- I am a forgiving and loving person.
- I am responsible for my own spiritual growth.
- My strength comes from forgiveness of those who hurt me.
- I am worthy of love.
- The more I love, the more love is returned to me.
- Love is eternal.
- I nurture my inner child, love it, and have allowed it to heal.
- I am responsible for my life and always maintain the power to be positive and have joy.

To visualize what you want is to have it. That may seem a simple task or, perhaps, a childish view of life. Neither is true. Although the simplicity is inherent in the belief of manifesting your destiny, the life you live to do it is not. It is a belief you live out of love and truth. Childish? Yes and no. It is getting back to the child-*like* wonder that the world is full of love and caring. But it is not a simplistic, or simple, vision of life. You must believe you can see what it is you want. The technique is simple, but the task is not unless you *truly believe* in yourself and know you can change and manifest what you want.

Visualizations are images we create in our mind. The word means, literally, to see in your mind. Your mind makes mental movies you will play over and over again. Our brain and its subconscious functions remember the things we see—a baby's smile, an amazing sunset, rain after a long dry spell. Of course we also see the homeless, traffic accidents, and crime. Our goal is to use images that create a mind set for positive action. We can recreate these images over and over again in our minds. Creating these mental movies of what we want does the same thing. The data is entered directly into our subconscious as having actually been *seen*. It is real to our brains. We have actually seen the images we created, therefore, creating the reality we want.

Seeing is believing. We *believe* what our eyes see. This is true for visual seeing as well as mental seeing. As you create an image in your mind, your brain believes it is happening and real. Repetition of the vision causes the image to become more real. Your mind begins to believe it actually has happened. The event has taken place. Combined with affirmations, it becomes a powerful tool to create what you want.

Set aside a time and place for meditation, visualization, and affirmations. This is best done at the same time every day. The more you practice, the clearer the images become. Always try to picture the same images every day, adding more detail as you become more comfortable with the process. View the pictures in your mind as a movie, with yourself as the lead actor.

Prepare an area, get into a comfortable position and close your eyes. See yourself awakening in the morning, stretching and smiling at the start of a new day. Get out of bed, make your coffee, tea or other morning beverage. See yourself sitting at the table smiling and enjoying it. Now, see yourself going to the bathroom, showering or bathing, and getting dressed. Hear yourself welcoming the new day. See yourself leaving for work or beginning your household chores. See the bounce in your step as you start a new and glorious day.

Raising children is one of life's most difficult enterprises. Parents can use all the help and support they can get, including affirmations.

Affirmations for parents:

- I am a loving parent. I seek at all times to do what is best for my child.
- I strive to raise my children to be free and independent.
- I teach my children the value of everyone around them.
- My children desire to leave the world a bit richer for their having been here.
- I teach my children to respect and value their elders.
- I am raising my children to be responsible citizens of the world.
- I am promoting the value of peaceful resolution to problems.
- I take time every day to connect and talk with my children.
- I recognize my children as unique individuals.
- I am forging bonds with my children now, which we will all desire to maintain, even when they are grown.
- My children recognize and appreciate what I do for them.

● I teach my children the importance of being a family, by my example as well as by my words.

In the kingdom of hope there is no winter.

—Russian Proverb

Even the most loved children have parents with the basic frailty of being human—they make mistakes. We can do our children a great service if we acknowledge this. If we teach them the power of making their own affirmations, we give them a tool they can use to help themselves. It will foster compassion and forgiveness for any mistakes you make, as well as appreciation for your efforts on their behalf.

Affirmations for children:
● I am loved for who I am, not for my accomplishments.
● I try to do my best at school and at home. I am working on becoming the best citizen I can be.
● I recognize my parents as people who love and care for me.
● I have concerns for other people in the world, beyond the borders of my own country.
● I spare others from harm or shame.
● I help my neighbors and my parents whenever I can.
● I listen to older people because they have much to teach me.
● I enjoy being active. I love my body for being fit and healthy.
● I will strive to get more sleep.
● I am organized and on task.
● I raise my hand in class. The teacher knows I am prepared and I value her instruction and guidance.
● I look out for children younger than I am.

Children often spend more waking time with their teachers than they do with their parents. Increasingly, schools are being asked to take on more and more tasks with regards to children. Teachers are often the front line of defense, too, when it comes to our kids. We need to support them and work as partners with them in raising and educating our young people.

Teachers, if you didn't already know, you're a hero! A child (or more than one), somewhere, knows how much you've changed their life and won't forget you. That child might be showing you now. Maybe they will show you in the future.

Affirmations for teachers:
- I make a difference.
- I touch the future every day.
- I do what many cannot do: I help children.
- I make sacrifices others will never know, and I do it with an open heart.
- I learn from my students.
- I value each of my students for their unique qualities.
- I plan my lessons carefully and thoughtfully.
- I involve my students in their education.
- I am creative and energetic in my teaching.
- I heed the wisdom of my fellow teachers. We have much to share with each other.
- I teach because it is where I can give the most of myself.
- I am sensitive to the needs of my students.
- I look for what my students don't tell me, as well as what they do.
- I touch the future because I teach.
- I make a difference!

Healthcare workers have a big responsibility. There's a great deal of truth in the old saying "if you don't have your health, you don't have anything." Working with people in any healthcare setting is a challenge. Working with people who are very ill can be even more so.

Affirmations for healthcare providers:
- I am skilled at what I do.
- Patients look to me for guidance and help.
- I am strong and ready to help people.
- I am reliable. My fellow healthcare professionals know they can depend on me.
- I work hard and continue to learn so I am always improving my skill.
- I am patient when people are in distress.

● I am calm and soothing to those who are in need.

TRY THIS

For older learners and adults: Create affirmations for your profession. Then create them for any profession other than your own—put yourself in another's shoes by focusing on the skills others need to do their jobs. If you perceive certain other jobs do not require skills, imagine doing their job. Perhaps the perception others have of that job is the biggest challenge the person in that position faces. Would you be willing to do their job?

For younger learners: Modify the exercise slightly by getting out those dress-up items again. Help students choose occupation-appropriate attire and act out jobs. Have them determine what duties the job might entail and what someone doing the job would need to do in order to excel at the job.

Confidence is that feeling by which the mind embarks in great and honorable courses with a sure hope and trust in itself.

—Cicero

I took a job preparation class once and a guest speaker came to make a presentation. He talked about affirmations, and we all had to write some. It sounded bogus to me, but I had been raised to be practical, and this sounded like junk. It wasn't real. And then, too, part of my attitude was to this guy. He was just a salesman, you know? I couldn't believe him. I did the exercises anyway, and I kept at it because I'm stubborn. I'm still not so sure about affirmations, but I keep working with them because at least it dug me out of being negative all the time. I can find something positive now most of the time, even when things seem really bad. Maybe they do work!

—Maureen T.

Affirmations for friends—after all, where would we be without them?

● I value our friendship because my friends and I complement each other.
● I cherish my friends because we share our lives.
● My friends support me when I need help.
● My friends can count on me if they need me.
● I am a good friend because I consider others feelings.

- I tell my friends often how important they are in my life.
- My friends enrich my life and make me a better person.

Affirmations are important to us as individuals. They can empower us, rouse us to believe in the possibilities we each contain. Empowered individuals want to promote the same feeling in their friends and associates. When everyone in your circle believes in their possibilities, more things get accomplished. Can we pass this idea along in our everyday lives? Of course. You might say it's another way of living the golden rule. How can you do this with people you don't know? It's not as hard as you think. Here are some general affirmations:

- I treat the people I encounter in my daily life with courtesy.
- Everyone can teach me something.
- I exercise extra patience with someone learning a new job.

Some Final Thoughts

The planning and writing of this book have taken me on quite a journey. I have discovered how to pinpoint my thoughts on the subjects we've explored here. By figuring out where conflicts arose as I worked with young people, I was able to develop concrete activities to help kids suffering from being labeled. I have found a stronger, more pro-active focus—one that will help me to help others who work with children.

I am more convinced than ever about the damaging effects of labeling. I am also encouraged that others share my views and are just as determined to start (or remain) on their own paths to effect change—one attitude at a time.

Our country is on the verge of grave, history-altering decisions. We face continuing challenges of feeding and caring for our homeless and elderly, educating our young people, and defining ourselves as Americans and citizens of the world. Increasingly, our young people will need to be ready particularly for the latter. We must train them to be responsible citizens of a global society. They cannot do this effectively if they have not been alerted to the dangers of labeling and how to interact with others using reasonable judgement, based on the merits of those with whom they are dealing.

I believe our youth are up to the challenge. I believe the responsibility lies with all of us to help and guide them. It is my hope this book has given you some insight, joy, and practical ways for making your life, and the lives of those you touch, better.

Index

A

AAUW. *See* American Association of University Women
Abbe, J.R. 5
Accelerated Schools Project 90
Adams, Henry Brooks 87
Affirmations
  for abundance 152
  for children 155
  for daily living 151
  for friends 157
  for health 151
  for health care providers 156
  for parents 154
  for peace and harmony 152
  for spirituality 153
  for students on health 152
  for teachers 156
  guidelines about 149
  samples of 146, 150
  use of to change attitudes 141-142
Aging. *See also* Elderly
Aging, myths about 134
Alda, Alan 123
Ali, Muhammad 66
Amabile, Teresa 94
Amazon.com 19
American Association of University Women 101, 102
American Psychological Association 10

Anger 47-48
  management 48
Apple Computer 19
Aristotle 126
Astaire, Fred 62

B

Baruch, Bernard 134
Beethoven 62
Belly and the Members, The 28
Bernstein, Leonard 51
Bezos, Jeff 19
Birth order
  how to change stereotypes of 39-41
  labeling 37-39
Bloom, Allan 83
Body image 71
Bonanza 66
Boundaries, setting 109-110
Bournemouth University 106
Brandeis University 94
Brown, Ronald 74
Bullying 10, 77
Bunyan, Paul 82
Bush, George W. 13
Butler, Samuel 28

C

Cal Poly 74
Caruso 62

Cervantes, Miguel de 142
Chan, Charlie 12
Charles, Ray 62
Chevalier, Maurice 131
Chicken and the Lake 74-75
Cicero 157
Clichés 63-65
Co-dependency 109-111
Cohen, Steve 89
Compassion 55
Compulsion 110-111
Confidence, projecting 67
Control in relationships 109-111
Cosby Show, The 12
cummings, e.e. 59, 67, 140

D

Diller, Phyllis 135
Disney, Walt 62, 139
Donne, John 18
Doolittle, Eliza 64
Durham, Bull 49

E

E is for Evidence 116
Einstein, Albert 24, 93, 144
Elderly, negative stereotyping of 127-131. See also Aging
Emerson, Ralph Waldo 76, 113
Epictetus 93
Equal Employment Opportunity Commission 123
Every Day Hero Award 70

F

Farquhar, Fay 53
Favoritism 30
Feldman, Robert S. 9
Fierstien, Harvey 144
Firearms, ownership of in U.S. households 7
Fort Worth Telegram 5
Fox and the Mask, The 49

Frank, Anne 151
Franklin, Benjamin 105, 141
Freud, Sigmund 117
Frost, Robert 85

G

Gandhi, Mahatma 65
Gardner, Dr. Howard 84
    types of learners 84
Gates, Bill 19
Gender bias. See Labeling, sexual stereotyping
Gide, Andre 108
Gifted children 92-94
Glass ceiling 8, 124
Godfather, The 56
Grafton, Sue 116

H

Hallam University 133
Harry Potter and the Chamber of Secrets 79

I

Individual Educational Plan (I.E.P.) 91
Irving, Washington 138

J

Jefferson, Thomas 81
Jeffords, Senator 13
Jobs, Steve 19
Johnson, Samuel 71
Journal of the American Medical Association 136

K

Keller, Helen 72, 138, 142, 150
King Leo 53-55

Index

L

Labeling
  and creation of confining boxes
    16-17
  in families 7, 28-48
    birth order, how to change
      stereotypes of 39-41
    birth order labeling 37-39
    parenting baseline 29-31
    parenting styles 41-42
  in the workplace 8
  need for 24
  reasons for 10-11
Labeling, choosing not to 138-158
  affirmations 146-148
    guidelines about 149
    use of to change attitudes 141-
      142
  visualization 143-145
Labeling, in school 74-95
  and teacher expectations 79-83
  bullying 77
  gifted children 92-94
  insults 77
  name-calling 77, 79
  standardized testing 87-89
  taunting 77
  teacher expectations 89-90
  teasing 77
    effects of 93
  test results, stakes attached to 87-
    88
Labeling, in the workplace 117-137
  sexual harassment 120-121, 123
Labeling, self-knowledge in 49-73
  clichés 63-65
  compassion 55
  self-concept 59-60
  self-esteem 51
  self-esteem and self-concept,
    difference between 56
Labeling, sexual stereotyping 96-116
  being single 115-116
  compulsion 110-111

gender bias, definition of 103
gender differences 112
language in 104
setting boundaries 109-110
sexual harassment 99-101
Labeling theory 7
Labels, creation of, ways for 27
Landon, Michael 66
Larkin, Philip 28
Learners, types of 84
Levin, Henry 90
Light, Professor Paul 106
Little House on the Prairie 66
Loukaitis, Barry 6

M

Me Cake 51
Meals on Wheels 149
Mencken, H.L. 49, 150
Meyrowitz, Joshua 127
Microsoft 19
My Fair Lady 64

N

Name-calling 8-9, 18, 77, 79
Nash, Ogden 31, 130
National Committee for Prevention
  of Child Abuse 48

P

Parenting baseline 29-31
Parenting styles 41-42
  assertive-democratic 41-42
  authoritarian 41-42
  permissive 41-42
  play 45
Peanuts 139
Play 45
Power in relationships 109-111
Puzo, Mario 56
Pygmalion 64

R

Rocky 67
Rostand, Edmond 149
Rowling, J.K. 79
Rudolph, Wilma 140

S

Saint-Exupery, Antoine de 103
Santana High School, shooting at 6, 9, 77
Schultz, Charles 139
Schweitzer, Albert 141
Science magazine 36
Self-concept 59-60
Self-esteem 51, 72-73
   and connection to body image 71
   ways to build 146
Self-esteem and self-concept, difference between 56
Self-fulfilling prophecy 64, 65
Senior citizens. *See* Elderly
Sesame Street 96
Sexual harassment 123
Sexual stereotyping. *See* Labeling, sexual stereotyping
Shaw, Bernard 64
Shaw, George Bernard 112
Sheboygan Area School District 107
Simonton, Dean Keith 95
Single, being 115-116
Slow Race 11
Smith, Stephanie 146
Sophocles 113
Spock, Dr. 35
Stallone, Sylvester 67
Standardized testing in schools 87-89
Stanford University 90
Steinem, Gloria 61
Stereotyping 10
   negative, of the elderly 127-131
Stevenson, Robert Louis 67

Strindberg, August 97
Sullivan, Annie 142
Superhero Awards 77
Supreme Court 120

T

Teacher expectations 89-90
Teasing 10, 77
Teasing, effects of 93
Television, influence on culture 11-12
Temple, Ed 140
Test results, stakes attached to 87-88
Theory of Multiple Intelligences 84
Thoreau, Henry David 5, 69, 71
Tierney, John 36
Trumpeter Taken Prisoner, The 13
Tufts University 89
Turtle's Race With Bear 14-16
Two Crabs, The 117

U

University of California 95
University of South Florida 64

V

Visualization 143-145, 153-154

W

Ward, Dr. Jack 133
Wepner, Chuck 66
Whitman, Walt 49
Wilde, Oscar 129
Williams, Andy 10
Williams, Charles "Andy" 6
Wise Men and the Elephant, The 5-6
Wolff, Virginia 96
World War II 42

Give the Gift of

Bigger Than the Box
The Effects of Labeling
to Your Friends and Colleagues

CHECK YOUR LEADING BOOKSTORE OR ORDER HERE

❏ **YES**, I want _____ copies of *Bigger Than the Box* at $19.95 each, plus $4.95 shipping per book (Ohio and South Dakota residents please add $1.25 sales tax per book). Canadian orders must be accompanied by a postal money order in U.S. funds. Allow 15 days for delivery.

❏ **YES**, I am interested in having Bonnie L. Haines speak or give a seminar to my company, association, school, or organization. Please send information.

My check or money order for $_____ is enclosed.

Please charge my: ❏ Visa ❏ Mastercard
❏ Discover ❏ American Express

Name _____

Organization _____

Address _____

City/State/Zip _____

Phone_____ E-mail _____

Credit card no. _____

Exp. date_____ Signature _____

Please make your check payable and return to:
BookMasters Distribution Center
30 Amberwood Pkwy. • Ashland, OH 44805
Call your credit card order to: (800) 247-6553
Fax: (419) 281-6883